M000201731

The Catalyst for Grace

Awakening to a Higher Love

Patricia Lea Ferrara

Copyright © 2016 by Patricia Lea Ferrara

All rights reserved. No part of this work may be reproduced by any mechanical, photographic, or electronic process, or in the form of a recording; or copied for public or private use (other than for "fair use" as brief quotations embodied in articles and reviews) without prior written permission of the author.

Ferrara, Patricia Lea
The Catalyst for Grace: Awakening to a Higher Love

Patricia Lea Ferrara—1st edition
Library of Congress Control Number: 2016940408

Published by PLF Press
Henderson, NV 89012
www.catalystforgrace.com

ISBN: 978-0-9975276-0-5 paperback
978-0-9975276-1-2 ebook
978-0-9975276-2-9 iBook

Cover Art: Win Ratz, www.winratzart.blogspot.com
Interior Dove Illustration: Peter Zarnoti

Design & Layout by

AquaZebra™
Web, Book & Print Design

www.AquaZebra.com

Printed in the United States of America.

Dedication

To the same One in all
in Whom we find
our real and eternal
existence

Author's Note

In 1976 I was awakened in the middle of the night with the words: "The Subject is Grace." I knew it was a book I was to write someday, but there was much I had to learn and experience first. This is that book, written after more than four decades of witnessing Grace, often in ways too sacred and astonishing to share. What is written here can only hint at what seems to lie beyond us that is reached within us.

Grace is a dimension of Consciousness that lies dormant until we awaken to our oneness with God, the Source and Essence of all that is real and eternal. However difficult or impossible the circumstances, Grace can break through any appearance and reveal a higher Love in operation. Most of the time our minds are closed, like a house with the doors and windows barricaded, and there is no room for Grace to enter.

Grace is always available, but the human identity is not the spiritual identity that is under Grace. We all know this, but have forgotten. We know our problems, faults, and diseases are not who we are. In fact, we suffer more because of the inconsistency between our true Self and the false sense of self with its failings, lacks, and vulnerabilities. We have forgotten the Soul. Like a dove tucked away in our heart of hearts waiting to be released so that it can fulfill its destiny, the Soul waits for us to yield ourselves so that Its fullness can come into expression. As the realization deepens that the *I* of our being is one with the Essence of everything, we become witnesses of Grace operating in natural and supernatural ways.

There is only one Creative Principle, God, Spirit, Soul. When experienced, It so completely infuses you that you realize It *is* you, but not the person you thought you were. You feel an expansion of being that is one with an all-knowing Intelligence and Love that fills all space. Once revealed, you want only what is *real* in Spirit and in Truth, for nothing else will satisfy on a spiritual journey that never ends.

Patricia Lea Ferrara
Henderson, Nevada

Table of Contents

INTRODUCTION:
A Spiritual Awakening

*That his prayer was nothing else but a sense
of the presence of God, his soul... insensible to
everything but divine love.*

Brother Lawrence[1]

Everyone who has a spiritual awakening remembers the moment when veils in the mind fall away and the Eternal reveals Itself. While this book is about Grace, not my personal life, it needs a beginning. For me that was June 24, 1969, in Minneapolis, Minnesota, when a veil was lifted and I came into the presence of God, which was unlike anything I had been taught.

A few years earlier I had come to the realization that the religion of my youth had failed to reveal evidence of a loving Creator. My prayers had gone unanswered, and the world had witnessed the assassinations of President Kennedy, Martin Luther King, and Robert

Kennedy, despite the prayers of millions. I no longer believed in a God who answered prayer. I had become an agnostic.

Perhaps because I had no religious beliefs at the time, there were no barriers, for the more rigid our beliefs about anything, the more opaque are the veils. The gift of faith is a spiritual impulse, an openness and responsiveness to the Divine. Once we *see*, faith is not blind, but an absolute conviction in what is revealed. Signs follow, but the Source remains hidden.

The Circumstances

Five days earlier I had been induced to give birth a month early to a seriously ill Rh[2] baby in an attempt to save his life. Neither obstetrician in two earlier pregnancies told me I was Rh negative, so I was totally unprepared when told this baby could be severely damaged and die inside of me during the pregnancy. I learned Rh symptoms are more severe in future pregnancies, so this was my last chance to have another child.

We were elated the baby survived his birth, but his heart stopped during a transfusion to exchange his blood. They were able to restart his tiny, premature heart, but it was too weak for the procedure that was necessary to save his life. Instead, he was placed in an incubator under bright lights with thick pads over his eyes to protect his vision. Phototherapy helps in lesser cases; he got worse. On the fifth morning the doctor told me to prepare for my baby's death. The toxic substance in his blood would soon cause organ damage. The only way to avoid it would be to re-attempt the transfusion, although his body was much weaker now than when it was tried after his birth. The transfusion was scheduled for the end of the day.

Overwhelmed with grief, I went to the intensive-care nursery to stare at the baby whose eyes I had seen only once, when I was allowed to hold him for less than a minute before he was placed in the incubator. As I left the nursery, I asked the nurse if there was a chapel near the maternity ward. I did not go there to pray. I needed a quiet place to prepare for the loss of my child.

The Mystery

Sitting in the empty chapel, I realized my baby was no more important than any child whose life is in danger. Whether children were dying in a hospital, starving in a poverty-stricken country or victims of war, there was no "God" intervening to save them. Later I came to see that God's work is already done: spiritual creation is complete. The problem is that we are not allowing the Grace that is ours and equally everyone's to flow.

That morning I sat in the chapel without faith, hope or belief. As I considered my life, I reached a point of unconditional surrender with the thought: "I do not know what

I have done that has brought me to these circumstances, but if there is a God, I surrender." Instantly, as if a camera lens opened in my awareness with no filters to block the light, I found myself face-to-face with an all-knowing Presence that fills all space. I did not see anything with my eyes: I *knew*, and I knew this Presence held me in perfect love throughout eternity, despite what was happening in the temporal scene.

The God that revealed Itself was unlike anything I had been taught. It was not a heavenly "Father" or "Person" or any spiritual identity or entity, but an all-encompassing Intelligence and Love in which I was included. I knew I existed in and of this Presence that knew me more intimately than I knew myself. I was also aware that I had existed *before* and would exist *after*, and that anything that seems to overwhelm us in life is insignificant compared to our eternal existence. At the time I still believed in the possibility of an afterlife, but pre-existence had never entered my mind.

Equally shocking was discovering that there was no Jesus between the Godhead and me, which was unlike everything I had been taught since childhood. Yet the words of Jesus came alive that moment, for I was shown that I too "am in the Father and the Father in me,"[3] although the "Father is greater than I."[4] It was easy to understand why Jesus called this loving Presence "Abba," an intimate, loving Aramaic term for

"Father," and acknowledged that It is greater than any of Its expressions, including himself.

The experience seemed as natural as opening dark curtains and letting sunlight into a room. I knew I had been shown what everyone knows, but has forgotten. We have forgotten our oneness with the Source and Substance of all that is real and eternal. Although there was no mediator between the Source and myself, in time Jesus and other illumined beings became living experiences, as they are and have been to many throughout the centuries.

The Miracle

When I left the chapel, I passed the intensive care nursery without going inside, although I did not expect to see my baby alive again. The awareness of my real existence "in God" was so strong, it erased all concern. Like Brother Lawrence, I was *"insensible to everything but divine love."*

I returned to my hospital room and fell into a deep sleep, emotionally drained by the doctor's report and mentally empty after the God experience. A few hours later two nurses woke me with tears running down their faces. "Your baby is all right." they said. "The doctor did not have to do the transfusion." The toxic blood condition that had risen for five consecutive days had suddenly dropped, and the baby was no longer in danger. It was 20 minutes before the scheduled procedure.

I had not prayed for my baby to be healed, but I knew intuitively that my experience in the chapel was linked to his recovery. Later I met many around the world who experienced the same Presence with signs following. Some saw a Light brighter than the sun; some heard a Voice. Others found themselves embraced in peace in the midst of danger or life-threatening symptoms. All experienced transformation and healing, though not always physical healing.

A Universal Experience

Nearly all who are touched by the Spirit find themselves profoundly changed and dedicated to a spiritual purpose, however unrecognized or recognized in the world. False appetites, material desires, and negative behaviors fall away. Some cannot smoke or drink again. They cease to use or enjoy vulgar language and entertainment. Many find their work and relationships change. Several experience physical or emotional healings or the dissolution of discordant circumstances. Others experience a deep peace before dying. It matters, for we take ourselves with us when we pass on.

Two who became close friends were struck to the floor in the echo of what seemed to them an audible Voice that thundered, **"I AM."** One was huddled under a table in the basement during a tornado, which destroyed the bookstore above her that had been a lifelong dream and scheduled to open the next day. The other lived alone and lay on the floor for hours after falling and breaking her hip. Nothing mattered compared to the Presence they had experienced that transformed their perception and their lives.

In the years that followed, I was to find the same Presence revealed in inspired verses of the Bible and the forbidden texts of Gnostic Christians; in Buddhism, Vedanta, and Taoism; in the teachings of Eastern gurus and Western mystics, and in mystical poetry. The interpretations and terminology differ, but the same Essence is revealed wherever anyone experiences pure Consciousness, Soul, or Spirit. It is a knowing beyond conditioned beliefs. Only in the Infinite Way message of Joel S. Goldsmith[5] did I find the explanation of my God experience and the healing that followed. Even more important, his books and recordings teach how to dwell in the awareness of a spiritual Presence that brings Grace into our lives as a continuing and deepening experience.

Whenever the Spirit touches us, Grace is released as peace, harmony, and wholeness, or an assurance that all is well despite what is happening in the temporal plane. You cannot swim in a lake without getting wet or stand in the sun without coming under its rays. Grace operates through us and for us, always for a greater good.

Problems are transformed or lose their power over us when we turn to the Spirit within us that exists within everyone. We discover prayer is a two-way flow that occurs in the deepest part of ourselves between the Soul and its Source, which are ultimately revealed as *One.*

The same Spirit or dimension that revealed Itself to Jesus, Buddha, Moses, Abraham, Isaac, Lao Tzu, Shankara, John, Paul, and all enlightened beings holds you in Its radiance now. The deeper experiences can never be shared, for no one can reveal the Eternal to another. The best anyone can do is to point the way, while this Presence waits to be acknowledged and embraced within yourself.

1

The Path of Oneness

Not as the branch is one with the tree,
but as a tree is one with its own nature.

An Inner Voice

The spiritual path is a way of life that appears when we are ready. It is as if invisible hands reach out to guide us by a way we could not have known, for it reveals another dimension. No one would walk this way unless prompted by a spiritual impulse; no one would know it exists. While it offers no material incentives, the benefits are unlimited and appear in tangible form.

When Spirit enters our lives, our values change. Once we experience a Presence that knows all things and is the *reality* of all being, we realize judging by appearances is never the truth about anything. We want only to follow the path that leads to greater spiritual awareness.

The Ultimate Surprise

Sometime in our existence we make choices that prepare us for the spiritual journey. Those choices link us with experiences, persons, and places beyond our imaginings. Though they may live thousands of miles away, we meet those with whom we share a spiritual bond or mutual purpose for good. We also come under the guidance of enlightened beings who may no longer live on the temporal plane, for neither time nor space is a barrier on the spiritual path.

What begins as a sole traveler in unfamiliar territory is like Dorothy starting out on the Yellow Brick Road, having no idea what lies ahead. Instead of the disappointments that hide behind the world's grand facades, we find ourselves one with an all-knowing Intelligence and Love. We become aware of the hollowness of relationships and activities that have no spiritual basis. It has nothing to do with religious beliefs or the lack of them, but with an underlying spiritual current.

The journey is amazing, but not always easy. There are times when everyone feels adrift on seas that are peaceful and glorious one day, turbulent and frightening the next, sometimes with no rescue in sight. Those on a spiritual path face the same challenges as the rest of the world, but find themselves upheld in the midst of the storms. Regardless of how overwhelming the waves, they come out afloat. The deeper the realization that there are no spiritual laws sustaining evil, the quicker the waves of discord, distress, lack, and disease break upon the shores of Spirit. Appearances are deceiving. Often what appears as harmony on the surface is far from the truth, and the turbulence is part of a cleansing process to remove the barriers to true peace. There can be no lasting harmony where we are not at peace within ourselves, for the Soul is a state of perfect peace.

Perhaps the ultimate surprise is the realization that everything in our lives is governed by our acceptance or rejection of the Essence that constitutes all being. Beliefs in separation from God, our real Self, and the rest of humanity have become so ingrained that the truth is denied and the lies believed. Deep down we know better but ignore the warnings until something jars us into awakening.

Laying Our Own Tracks

There are no brightly lit highways or enticing billboards on the spiritual path, but there are spiritual principles that guide us like road signs along the way. The principles are the same for everyone, but we can only travel the path that individually unfolds. Every spiritual principle or "road sign" points to a deeper awareness of *One*: One Presence, One Power, One Life; One Spirit, One Substance, One Soul. To contemplate the nature of God as One lifts us above the physical sense of life into an inner space where Grace functions.

Unless we establish spiritual truth in our awareness, we are still governed by a material sense of life. Nothing enters our lives without first being accepted in our awareness. Even subconscious contents have been accepted at some level of consciousness. Only when the truth is known are false beliefs flushed out or not allowed entrance. As we go deeper into meditation and the practice of spiritual principles, we respond less and less to the beliefs that assault mind, body, relationships, and supply. We think we have found the secret of life and we have, but we soon discover why so few travel the spiritual path.

Many years ago I was shown in a dream how we lose the way. I saw a trail leading straight to an individual's fulfillment. Then I saw a person laying her own tracks, like a train engine that lays its tracks as it moves forward. As the person wandered slightly off the trail, I saw with a shock that even the slightest change in direction ends up far from the intended destination. At first we may not realize we have meandered off the path, for the ego's methods are subtle and its subterfuges engaging. No matter how far off the trail we go, there is always a way back. Everyone is free to turn within to a higher Power because freedom is a Soul quality. No one can rob another of a Soul quality. That is why there will always be uprisings against those who try.

Before we awaken, it is easy to get sucked into the ego's traps. As we struggle to climb out of the pits we fell into because we left the trail to lay our own tracks, we learn to step more cautiously. If we are willing, an indwelling Spirit will expose the masquerades that parade before us in forms both alluring and ugly. Grace takes over when the desire for truth is greater than any attachment or repulsion to form. My dream was an awakening and a warning. Trust your innermost Self and the Source that animates it, and the trail you follow will be straight.

Never Our Responsibility

Every spiritual realization reveals more of a dimension unlimited in scope and effects. When Spirit initiates a task, we are given the capacity to fulfill it, but the responsibility for the outcome is never on our shoulders. That which gives the work will fulfill it if the personal sense of self gets out of the way. Spirit operates not merely *as* us—that may be the smallest part—but *through* us. Personalizing cuts off the flow of a Presence whose reach is infinite. Only the ego personalizes.

So what do we do when the burdens seem to fall on our shoulders? "We live amid surfaces and the true art of life is to skate well on them."[1] Professional skaters keep their balance on the ice and their blades sharp. They train hard, but do not feel responsible for the sky above or the ice below. They just skate the best they can. We too have to "skate" the best we can, without entertaining a false sense of responsibility for the outcome. We have to keep our awareness sharp, while maintaining a balance between our inner and outer lives.

As we realize we are one with an infinite Source and do our best to skate well upon the surfaces in our lives, we discover we are supported by an invisible Presence that not only governs our actions, but also the sky above and the ice below. While some persons appear to fall through holes in the ice, in a future time or dimension everyone will awaken into the awareness of divine love. The challenges never end because the world will always present appearances that deny the allness of love. It is part of the changing temporal scene, but not part of an all-spiritual universe governed by Grace.

The way to come under Grace is to drop the temporal sense of life and realize your oneness with God. If that is too great a leap, realize oneness with your own essence for there is only one Essence. To consciously dwell in the Essence that runs through everything is to feel Its peace and become part of the world's solutions, rather than feed its problems. It is true that we have to give up the world to find what is not of the world, but that has to do with detachment, not asceticism. Attachment binds us to the ego and laws of earth, while Grace transcends physical and karmic laws.

Close your eyes for the next few moments and throw your invisible arms wide open without resistance or desire. Let the allness of Spirit permeate your mind and your body, your nights and your days. Do it often, until it becomes as natural as breathing, and never separate your spiritual practice from your daily activities. Your life will change because consciousness and its effects are one. The world will still present attractions and disturbances, but they will no longer entrap or fool you for long.

No Greater Gift

There is no greater gift than to find ourselves held in an infinitely loving Presence that knows us better than we know ourselves and has already provided for our bliss. The blessings that come on the spiritual path are greater than any temporary good or passing hardship. Those who think the spiritual path is hard make their belief a law unto themselves. It is the world that is hard, not God.

There are many spiritual paths leading to the top of the mountain. Although they differ in language, form, and practice, all true paths lead to the same destination at the highest elevation because there is only One. If we accept the invitations that Spirit presents, we find the best route from where we are at the moment to the Soul's fullest expression. As we practice meditation and listen within ourselves, we touch an inner current that not only guides our footsteps, but also makes the right connections for the fullness of Soul to manifest. It can take time to undo or resolve the errors we have made, but if we are true to our highest awareness, Grace abounds and eases the journey.

Illuminations come along the way in flashes of insight, moments of perfect peace, and amazing happenings. The spiritual path culminates in the realization that our oneness with God is not only as a branch is one with the tree, but also *as a tree is one with its own nature.* What that means is only revealed as you turn within and experience it yourself.

2

Unto Ourselves

Whose sins you shall forgive,
they are forgiven you—in you.

Whose sins you shall retain,
they are retained—in you.

As I walked among the wildflowers at a retreat center in the 1980s, an inner Voice spoke the above words
as softly as the petals that brushed my ankles. It is the
atmosphere of a place that makes it holy. Any space
dedicated to a spiritual purpose where contemplation and universal love are practiced exudes a sacred
silence that makes it easier to *hear* with an inner ear.
Similar words in the New Testament have been given
a different meaning: "whose sins you shall forgive, they
are forgiven *them*; whose sins you shall retain, they are
retained."[1] The meaning imparted to me that summer
day was not unto "them," but unto ourselves.

No Recrimination in Divine Love

When Spirit reveals Itself, it is always a revelation of love. We may not understand the implications at the time, but later we recognize the hand of Love governing, guiding, and appearing as good in our lives. We may respond with a jolt to Its revelations, but there is no recrimination in the purity of divine love. How do we know it is not imagination, psychic phenomena or a brain aberration, as skeptics always claim?

Whenever we hear the "still small voice,"[2] we recognize a Source that leaves no doubt of Its authority. There is clarity beyond ideas and beliefs, and the love is unmistakable. You know when it is true. You do not think you know; you *know*. The moment passes, but the awareness never leaves us. The same truths can be found in ancient civilizations, not because one culture transmitted it to a distant other, but because they receive it from the same Source. Truth reveals Itself to anyone receptive to Its call. Omnipresence is always revealing Itself; the barriers are in us, not out there. As we surrender to an inner Source, Grace dissolves the penalties for past mistakes and brings all things together for good.

Consciousness is precise. Either Grace is operating or we suffer from past transgressions and whatever current theories and beliefs we accept as true for the world and ourselves. Every false belief and unloving act bring consequences even if unintentional, just as every error in mathematics produces the wrong answer without conscious intent. The penalties continue until only love fills our awareness. It is a lifelong challenge. At first it may seem impossible to give up hatred, resentment, and vengeance because there is so much evidence in the world to justify these feelings. Yet when the Spirit touches us, we experience only the all-encompassing wisdom and love of an infinite Source. We have to be willing to give ourselves to the process. It has to do with priorities, not time. We all have the same 24 hours to open or close our minds to the Divine.

Divine love never deviates. We cannot experience the freedom of spiritual being without becoming one with the inflow and outflow of a Love that wants everyone to spiritually prosper. Jesus said to forgive not seven times but seventy times seven, which means to forgive everyone everything. Buddha said we are not punished for our anger but by our anger. They did not say it would be easy.

All we take with us when we depart this life is our state of consciousness. If we do not rid ourselves of negative feelings and behaviors now, we will have to learn the same lessons later. Eventually every offense will dissolve in the intensity of the Godhead. It may feel like unquenchable flames to those who resist the nature of God in themselves. Those who willingly surrender feel only the ecstasy of One.

Questions to Ask Ourselves

Since there is no one to be forgiven in divine love, why is forgiveness emphasized by all illumined beings? They experienced a Presence that emits only love because that is Its nature. They know that every unforgiving thought and unloving act separate us from the allness of Spirit and block the fullness of Grace in our lives.

To "forgive" means to pardon completely, wholly, without reservations. It does not mean to ignore or absolve monstrous acts or their perpetrators, or to personally love or allow abusive persons into our lives. Some acts are unforgiveable, but we can pray that all awaken to the same Source and love we recognize for ourselves. When we desire vengeance or retaliation toward others, we make it harder for them—and for us—to respond to Grace.

To come under Grace, we have to be willing to acknowledge our errors. We need to ask:

- ❧ What am I carrying in my mind and heart?
- ❧ Is this what I want to take with me when I depart this life?
- ❧ Is this what I want to leave behind or carry with me now?

Take a few minutes to inwardly face the person

or situation that most upsets you, the one you haven't wanted to think about or think about too much. Ask to see it as an impersonal observer, like watching a movie without entering the drama. Realize your mind is projecting these images, and your reaction is based solely upon your limited, subjective interpretation. It may or may not be true objectively and has nothing to do with the truth spiritually. When we sincerely ask to know the truth about a situation or person, whatever we need to know eventually comes to the surface. Nothing is hidden that will not be revealed on any level of life to those who are spiritually awake. It may not be easy to face what is revealed, but unless we do, we are living in an illusion. An illusion will never bring fulfillment.

If the ego protests in its own defense, meditate on the *I* of your being that is untouched by any negative act or circumstance until the peace that fills all spiritual space floods your awareness. When you rest in the peace of Soul, you find freedom from whatever is disturbing you and operating as a barrier to Grace in your life. Something good will happen. It may seem unrelated, but you will know a barrier dissolved in you and a higher Power took over. As your mind becomes a lighter, brighter place, it reflects in your world.

The Radiance of Being
Soul-centered individuals have a wider range of

influence due to the radiance of their being. Think not only of Jesus, Buddha, Jewish mystics, Eastern masters and Western saints, but also of the many unrecognized persons who may this moment be embracing you in their light.

Deeper than the ego-self is the Soul that is unchanging in Its essence and intentions. When we consciously rest in oneness with the part of us that lies beyond thought and emotion, we touch an inner radiance. It is the nature of the Soul to shine. You cannot turn on a lamp and confine the light to the bulb. Even a tiny candle illuminates the darkness, however minuscule its light. When the Soul lies dormant beneath the rumblings of the mind, the rays of Grace are blocked.

As we ponder Omnipresence in meditation and acknowledge It in whatever confronts us, the Soul begins to shine like the sun in ourselves and in those who enter our radius. We begin to sense a spiritual Presence everywhere. It has to be a daily practice because the world constantly presents appearances that deny an all-spiritual dimension governed by love. Those who abuse others violate themselves—the same Spirit in all—and will not escape their brutality until they too awaken to the radiance of being within everyone.

As spiritual love is realized in our awareness, it acts as a purifying agent in us and flows out into human consciousness, revealing the best in all who respond to a divine impulse. "Whose sins you shall forgive are forgiven *in you;* whose sins you shall retain are retained *in you.*" Our part is to remove the barriers within ourselves.

Fill me, flood me
With Thy grace,
That I might *be*
A holy place.

3

A Divine Persuasion

No man can conform his faith to the dictates of another. The life and essence of religion consist in the internal persuasion or belief of the mind.

Thomas Jefferson, 1776

Within everyone is an "internal persuasion" or natural inclination toward ultimate Truth. We never lose our essential nature, but we have identified with a false sense of self and forgotten who and what we are. When we enter the stillness of meditation, light enters dark caverns in the mind we did not know were there. We discover an inner frequency or tempo that is nothing like the human personality. We experience our true and eternal nature that exists beyond mind and body. The ego's worries and desires disappear in the revelation of spiritual being.

Many are forced off the ego's edge by adversity, but it can also happen in meditation and contemplative prayer.

If we consciously open ourselves to God, we discover we have always been one with an infinite Intelligence and Love, despite personal and world problems. The question then becomes: Is there a way to bring the Grace that governs an all-spiritual dimension into our lives in the world?

A Love Letter from God

Grace takes over when we surrender to a higher Power and are willing to make whatever adjustments are needed to become one with the nature of God in ourselves. Every violation causes a disturbance in our minds, bodies, and worlds, and clogs the channel to Grace. If we are to experience our spiritual heritage, we have to keep the channel open.

Spiritual surrender is like opening a love letter from God. The world's view of surrender implies submission to an outside force that has the power to deny our rights and desires. Spiritual surrender is to consciously yield to a Presence that sets us free and fulfills our true desires. It is not surrendering to a Zeus-like, Father-God whose will is opposed to our aspirations. It is the fulfillment of our highest aspirations by the Source that gave them to us.

The love letter opens when the mind is still, but how do we bring the contents into our lives? When we make meditation a regular practice, we enter the rhythm of Spirit where nothing needs to be improved, added, changed, or healed. The experience forms the basis of faith. Faith cannot be imposed by dogma or fear. It is often inspired by someone we learn about or meet, but it springs from an internal persuasion.

Trust the rhythm that arises from a wellspring of peace within you to reveal Grace in any situation. Grace does not differentiate whether it is for you, someone close to you, or a world situation, for what is held close in your heart is part of the consciousness you are.

> Be still my mind and rest
> in the rhythm of Soul,
> the peace of God that fills all space
> and reveals that there is no place
> where **I**, Spirit, am not.

In meditation a spiritual impulse permeates our minds, bodies, and worlds, unless it is blocked by false beliefs and behaviors. Everyone is under a belief in separation and duality until Grace reveals oneness with the Source that includes all good for all persons. Appearances that deny an all-loving Source persist, but only operate upon acceptance.

> Do **I** not fill heaven and earth, Spirit says,
> or do you accept a presence and
> power greater than **I AM**?

The love letter is always closer than breathing. Until we accept its contents, the fullness of Grace is dormant. It flows from a temple within ourselves.

Entering the Temple

Each time we enter the sanctuary of our own being, we enter a temple that welcomes us with peace, love, harmony, and wholeness.

Enter this door
As if the floor within were gold
And every wall of jewels,
All of wealth untold,
As if a choir
In robes of fire were singing here,
Nor shout, nor rush,
but hush, for
GOD is here.[1]

When Spirit is realized in an individual's awareness, a holy hush permeates the atmosphere. It can be felt in the presence of those who dedicate their lives to a spiritual purpose, and in churches, temples, and retreat centers dedicated to peace. It can be sensed where saints have lived, where American Indians and Australian Aborigines have worshipped, on the grounds of Christian and Buddhist monasteries, and in the ashrams of Eastern masters. Materialistic minds feel nothing but surfaces. Others feel an atmosphere of peace without understanding why. Those who are spiritually awake recognize the signs and the Source. Meditation is touching who and what we really are, not a dramatic leap into a strange psychic realm. Spirit is our true nature, and the temple is within ourselves.

Devoted men and women teach, guide, inspire, and comfort in religions around the world, but a belief in duality—God and devil, heaven and hell—still dominates religious thought. Throughout history individuals of all religions and those without religious ties have experienced pure Consciousness, God, a divine Source or Creative Principle. They did not find a God who condemns or a devil. As more people awaken to their oneness with God, more will experience Grace in their lives.

Jesus said: "Woe unto you, lawyers! for ye have taken away the key of knowledge: ye entered not in yourselves, and them that were entering in, ye hindered."[2] He was not referring to what we know as the legal profession today, but to those who try to enforce their interpretation of religious rules upon others. He not only accuses them of taking away *the key of knowledge* that gives everyone full access to God, but also of not *entering into themselves*—the only place where God or Truth is experienced—and hindering those who do.

Revealed truth always survives, as it has with the Nag Hammadi codices[3] hidden 17 centuries ago when Christian church leaders condemned Gnosticism. Those who hid these writings felt they were important enough to risk excommunication, public censure, and punishment. They knew the way to know God is through self-knowledge or "gnosis," and that it is possible for all who seek it within themselves. Mystics in every age and culture have known this. Revealed truth translated by scholars without religious bias is often the catalyst for mystical awareness, but the truth still remains hidden unless revealed by the Spirit within you.

Revelation is an instantaneous knowing. The moment passes, but the impact is life changing unless a strong sense of ego persists. Eventually suffering will cause the ego in everyone to yield, but it does not have to happen through suffering. Close your eyes and dive deep into yourself now. Feel the expansiveness of your own being that reaches beyond time and space, body and mind. There is no ego there. The ego does not automatically dissolve at death; only the form changes. The form will continue to change until there is only the individual expression of Spirit without the erroneous beliefs and behaviors with which we have identified.

The Real Body
Illumined beings remain a living presence after

their deaths because they have realized their incorporeality and entertain no separation between God and themselves. No longer bound by a belief in physicality, they are available to all who seek their help. This was true before their deaths too, but their followers could not see beyond the physical form. Instead of realizing the same Spirit in themselves, they worshipped the messenger without catching the message.

Jesus had to tell his followers: "if I go not away, the Comforter will not come unto you."[4] The Comforter is the Spirit of God in everyone. Whether eternal truths are transmitted through an illumined being or directly from an infinite Source, there is only one Mind revealing Itself to Itself. When truth is revealed through illumined beings, it is their enlightened awareness that reaches us, not their personalities or bodies.

Those who believe the physical body will rise are stuck in duality and dogma. The real body will rise because it is not and has never been physical. It has always been spiritual and eternal, or Omnipresence is not real. As an inner Voice said to me: *"Death is not only not inevitable, it is impossible."* When we realize Spirit as the only presence, physical conditions have less power in our experience. No one can avoid them altogether, but many have seen an invisible Power prevent or nullify negative conditions after an experience of Oneness, "heaven," Christ, angels or a spiritual Presence.

Just as the real body is not physical, the real world is not material. World work is an important part of spiritual practice, but the prayer that dissolves evils is not the prayer of petition, as if a God is withholding his blessings and can be influenced by us to release them. Rather, it requires spiritual work within us to realize a dimension where Grace has never ceased. It may require the unity of national leaders to stop wars, but peace cannot last unless the same Spirit in all is recognized in the hearts of the people. If spiritual awakening were a universal experience, war, prejudice, and injustice would be impossible.

Those who do spiritual work for the world have seen evils stopped in their tracks, or made evident so they can be stopped, or a greater good result from what looks like a great injustice or tragedy. It requires constant vigilance on our part to realize the omnipresence of Grace. Grace is more powerful than any weapon and without collateral damage, but it must be realized to function in the three-dimensional world. As meditation deepens, we see the circumference of Grace expanding, unless the resistance is too great.

The Stream of Non-Resistance

Jesus taught "Resist not evil,"[5] but rarely is the lesson explained. Grace operates like Lao Tzu's example of a little stream that winds its way down mountains, over rocks, and through narrow crevices, reaching its goal without resisting obstacles. We have to be like that little stream, letting nothing block our recognition of Omnipresence. Where evils are resisted or accepted as inevitable, Grace is blocked.

Resistance is a rope that keeps us bound. The more we resist a person or condition, the more we endow it with power. You feel it when your body tenses up against someone or something. To relax and get into an inner flow opens the way for Grace to function. Non-resistance is a spiritual practice. It means to rest in the awareness of Spirit as the *only* presence, power, substance, activity, and law, despite what is appearing in our lives or the world. This is not a state of denial, indifference, or passivity, but attuning to a higher Truth.

Those who have benefited the world by their spirituality, service, or leadership were neither passive nor indifferent. They were strong and determined in their missions, but they also knew the greater works are accomplished with a peaceful heart that allows a higher Power to direct their actions and the outcome. When Soul speaks unto Soul, Oneness rather than divisiveness is felt and externalizes as whatever is needed for good. Only the ego resists and connives; the Soul abides in perfect peace.

Rest like a wave—
without fear,
without hope—
in an Ocean of peace
beyond its endurance,
For the Soul rests in God
with total assurance.

Finding Your Purpose

The Infinite has no favorites. What appears as greater blessings may not be as it seems, or may be evidence of a person's spiritual receptivity. Neither Jesus nor Buddha said the rest of us are inferior in our essence. Our inferiority lies in our ignorance and behaviors. Whatever degree of belief in a presence, power or law apart from Spirit is the degree we remain under physical and karmic law. Grace transcends both and reveals a higher law and purpose.

Those given a mission are protected in its fulfillment, despite persecution, obstacles, illnesses, and early deaths. Long after they pass from sight, they continue to be an influence for good. Spiritual awakening always reveals a higher purpose, and life does not end at the grave. Only the Spirit within you can reveal your purpose. All enlightened beings had to turn to the same Spirit within themselves. It is no less available now than it was then. Everyone has the same access.

Be still, so still that your breath
becomes an inflow and outflow of peace
from a Source deeper than mind,
body, or circumstance.

Drop all resistance and feel yourself
embraced in an Ocean of stillness,
carried on waves of Grace.

For some it will be an instantaneous awareness; for most it may take many attempts. Neither the timing, nor the effects are up to us. Our part is to open the inner door and rest there long enough to feel the stillness that permeates all being. If it does not happen the first, the fifth or the fiftieth time, keep trying. Eventually the Infinite will reveal Itself in some inconceivable way. It is an awareness that comes by Grace according to a divine persuasion.

4

Exceeding Fine

*The mills of the gods grind slowly,
but they grind exceeding fine.*

Ancient Greeks

When we follow a spiritual path, a refining process begins that never ends. At first it refines our outer lives as former interests, activities, and relationships fall away that are not in the divine design. Even our language and wardrobe may change to reflect a less worldly, more refined state of being. More important are the inner changes. It refines our values, behaviors, and use of time, for there is much to be refined in everyone.

For our lives to flourish by Grace, there must be no unloving thoughts. It seems impossible where a horrendous crime or grave injustice has occurred. Love never condones evil, yet we must find a way to dissolve our anger for the fullness of Grace to flow.

One Source, Many Faces

The truth goes beyond victim and perpetrator, innocence and guilt. The murderer, the terrorist, the child abuser, the thief, and their victims are not as they seem. Hidden behind every face is the same Source expressing Its infinite nature. Those who do not let that nature shine have blocked it within themselves.

Everyone has an eternal identity untouched by sin, disease, and death. When we spiritually awaken, we realize mortality is a false sense of life. We have forgotten our eternality and Omniscience, Omnipotence, and Omnipresence. The three "O's" have long been recognized by most religions, but are rarely realized or practiced. It is the realization and practice that reveal a higher Wisdom and Love operating in human affairs. It begins with our acknowledgment, but realization happens in the Soul.

This is not a denial of the evil that happens in the world everyday, or the personification of evil that can occur when the mind is open to psychic phenomena. When tragedy happens, it is real on the third-dimensional plane, but that does not make it spiritually *real.* To deny or ignore it does not help those in need of our support, so what are we to do? We have to look deeper than the world of duality and touch the deep well of peace within ourselves where Grace functions. If God were in the appearance world, nothing would happen outside of the omnipresence of love.

Judging by appearances never reveals the truth about a person or situation unless we see with spiritual discernment or an intuitive sense. When we realize appearances are deceptive, we learn not to react with excessive anger, fear or elation. The goal is to stay consciously receptive to a higher Power, while supportive of those who need our help. In any situation we can ask in prayer and meditation for the spiritual truth to be revealed. Then we witness Grace blessing persons and transforming situations in inexplicable ways, but the real transformation occurs within us.

The Veil Removed

When we dedicate ourselves to the spiritual path, we have experiences that all illumined beings describe, including the challenges that are part of a "refining" process. It is not easy to realize Grace when faced with evil, but that is the work of every spiritual initiate. That was my work in 2004 when I was unable to release my anger against those who caused the deaths of nearly 200 young children on their first day of school in Beslan.

When you read this, there will be another terrorist group, dictator or bully threatening world peace and individual freedoms. The lesson applies, whether the enemy is national, international or personal. When hatred, vengeance or indignation rise up within us, it is never a Soul response. As I watched the terrified children in Beslan on TV before the explosions that killed many of them, I felt my anger like a tight knot that kept me from reaching the stillness that usually enveloped me in meditation, yet I could not deny my feelings. You cannot fool yourself or Omniscience.

In the midst of the crisis, an inner Voice spoke:

> *Forgiveness is the way to live,*
> *They know not what they do, forgive.*

I was stunned to recognize Jesus speaking and at the depth of love behind his words. The tenderness in his voice was beyond description. There was no judgment toward those responsible for the children's deaths, or of me for my anger, only a love that equally embraced all. Then I heard myself respond from a depth in myself I did not know existed:

> *Forgiveness, Lord, help me to see,*
> *Forgiving them, forgiving me.*

Forgiving *me?* How could I be compared to those responsible for killing and terrorizing hundreds of children, their teachers and the parents held captive inside the school? Didn't they deserve my rage? What about the grieving families and traumatized children who escaped? None of the ego's arguments mattered, for the love I was shown was beyond explanation.

A Knot Dissolves

If we are to know God, there must be no chinks in our armor of oneness. Whatever needs to be refined in us dissolves or comes to the surface to be corrected. Sometimes similar circumstances give us the opportunity to act differently. Other times acknowledging our violation is enough for the humility that allows the correction to occur.

Every transgression leaves an imprint upon us that operates until it is dissolved or corrected. We have no idea of the forces that govern us or how we set them in motion until we awaken to the love that knows no exceptions. The filter is finer for those who should know better. Even indifference can be a serious violation.

We have all heard that our lives flash before us when we die. It can also happen when we are alive and well. It is like watching a movie where you are the main character and witnessing yourself as the villain, even if you had no awareness of your transgressions at the time. We witness those hurt by our actions or refusal to act. It is part of the refining process and never easy to face. In the midst of my anger at the Beslan terrorists, I was shown an incident that was never in my conscious memory. I was horrified to watch my indifference toward a little girl in my fourth grade class who wore a wig and had no eyebrows or eyelashes. At the time she seemed an oddity of nature. It never occurred to me that she may have had cancer and lost her hair from chemotherapy, for in those days children knew nothing about such things.

It did not matter that I was ignorant, that it happened more than 50 years earlier, or that we never actually met. What mattered was that I had not reached out with love to a child who had surely suffered and perhaps died soon, for she was in my school for less than a month. "They know not what they do," the Voice had said about those who were indifferent to the children they took as hostages. Neither did I recall my own indifference toward a child until forced to look at it. None of us know how often we violate the law of love. Never doubt you will be shown your transgressions and discover you are your own and harshest judge.

Only when I acknowledged my indifference toward the little girl in my school did the knot in my chest open, like a tightly closed bud opening to the sun. Where there had been outrage, there was only compassion for the misguided young militants whose plans had gone amok. They believed they were freedom fighters in an unjust war and must have felt their actions were the best way to be heard. Whether they set off the explosions that killed those held captive for more than two days without food or water in a stifling gymnasium, or it was gunfire from the rescuers, the hostage-takers were responsible for the terror, killings, and more than 300 deaths from the explosions.

The love I was shown did not justify their actions, but that was not the point. He told me: "They *know not* what they do, *forgive.*" There was no "eye for an eye," everlasting hell, temporary purgatory, or karmic retribution. That which is the nature of God does not want anyone to suffer for any reason, rather that all awaken into the allness of divine love. Only the ego seeks retaliation.

Become a Catalyst for Grace

Regardless of how evil anyone may seem, everyone has the potential to be an instrument for Grace. One person's silent recognition can be the catalyst that spiritually awakens others or dissolves or exposes evil. We have no idea how far-reaching the effects when we become an inlet and an outlet for a love far greater than ours.

It is impossible not to be angry at torture, murder, tyranny, greed, and injustice, yet if we are willing, Spirit flushes away all unlike Itself and reveals Grace in the darkest corners. It does not mean allowing criminals and terrorists to get away with acts against humanity or to free them to commit more heinous acts. It means to make space in our minds and hearts for Grace to operate through us and through them too, even if they are rightly sentenced to prison for life. In any situation we can remain estranged or melt into a Source that freely offers Its love to all.

"The mills of the gods grind slowly but they grind exceeding fine." Somewhere there is a tally that we will face in ourselves against the standard of divine love. When we are ready, an unseen Power arranges what is necessary to dissolve knots in us we do not know are there. Our response to what is happening on the sidelines of our lives can be as important as the major events. That I was a child myself with no awareness of having done anything wrong was not acceptable. What may be accepted as the norm for any age is not the norm for spiritual being.

Whatever is happening on the surface of your life, something more is happening on a deeper level. Watching the Beslan school crisis and the long row of dead children in open caskets on BBC-TV in London in total silence, without the interruption of TV commentators and commercials, enabled me to hear an inner broadcast. I had no idea "the mills of the gods" were grinding on me to dissolve an old transgression and reveal a finer aspect of love. I knew it was a lesson not meant for me alone.

Forgiveness is the way to live,
They know not what they do, forgive.

Forgiveness, Lord, help me to see
Forgiving them, forgiving me.

5

Always Speaking

Hear ye, hear ye, hear ye:
The Lord God Omnipotent reigneth.

An Inner Voice[1]

Recently someone on a popular television show said: "Beware of anyone who claims to hear God speak." We should be wary if we are *not* hearing God speak. The Soul of the universe is always speaking. It speaks through nature, a new friend, an old friend; a home that says "buy me"; a pet that says "take me home." It speaks through a poem, a song, or a book that transmits the awareness of a Love that never leaves or forsakes us.

Spirit speaks through any act or intention that spreads love, improves life, or elevates humanity. It speaks most profoundly in an experience of Oneness beyond any human relationship. When we realize there is nothing but Spirit, It speaks through everything. Yes, beware of those who set themselves up as special and claim an inner voice justifies their actions. Spirit initiates, invites, guides, reveals, bestows. Even when a spiritual impulse speaks as clarity, inspiration, or assurance, Spirit does not command, for that is not Its nature. Its purpose is always to reveal a higher Love.

First in Line

The love between Spirit and its expressions—the Father and the Son—does not differentiate. No matter how many have awakened before you or the degree of sin or denial, you are always first in line with God. Close your eyes and feel your innermost Self. It includes your first breath of life to the farthest star in your awareness and everything in-between, before and after. Look around "in there" and see if there is anything between you and your Soul. Nothing can enter there. It is only the mind that gets in the way.

When we are spiritually awake, it is as natural to sense a spiritual Presence as it is for someone attuned to nature to hear the birds and marvel at the night skies. If we are serious about knowing God or ultimate Truth, we have to develop our Soul capacities. The strings of the Soul never get brittle or play out of tune, but they need to be played to be heard. It happens in silence when we unplug from the mishmash of the mind and the world's noise. As we dwell in the peace that is the Soul's atmosphere, we come into alignment with

Grace—divine love in action—here and now.

Divine love is impersonal in the sense that it is universal, yet it is the most personal of all relationships because it transpires in the most intimate part of the Self. Regardless of how profound anyone's experience, it never detracts from another's in a realm where everyone is first in line. Rather, as each star brightens the night skies, each glimmer of spiritual truth makes it more accessible for all.

The Importance of Alertness

Spirit is always speaking, but our attention is elsewhere. We not only do not hear; we have also forgotten the listening apparatus. An intuitive sense is always present to guide us in the ways of love. It operates like an invisible antenna and needs no mental direction. Unless we are inwardly alert, we do not sense the *I* of our being that is always speaking and sensed in stillness.

Sometimes an original phrase or a familiar or unfamiliar quotation, lyric, or melody floats into the mind with a message for us in the moment. The words seem random, as if our stream of consciousness has picked up a few dead twigs. We ignore them or they pass by without recognition. These seemingly random thoughts and feelings are not dead twigs, but living branches extended to reveal a spiritual Presence that never leaves us. They come to lift our spirits, widen our horizons, and resolve or dissolve a dilemma. They come to restore our balance when something has knocked us off the beam, or as reassurance that all is well. All is always well *in God*, but most people do not consciously dwell there. It is a state of mind that is *wide-awake*.

Spiritual truths apply universally, but only when they register in us do they function for us. Sometimes what we inwardly hear or sense is only understood with deeper contemplation or research. For example, the words "every good and perfect gift" meant nothing to me when they welled up in meditation. Not finding the phrase in a book of literary quotations, I checked a Bible concordance and found it in James 1:17: *"Every good gift and every perfect gift is from above, and cometh down from the Father of lights, with whom there is no variableness, neither shadow of turning."* The moment I read the phrase in context with the rest of the verse, I had an instant release from a situation that had disturbed me for months.

The particulars do not matter, except as an example to be alert to the Soul's stirrings. When spiritual truth is revealed in us, we find clarity where there was confusion, peace where there was disturbance, and freedom where there was bondage. Negative conditions dissolve or no longer affect us, or the Grace is given us to deal with them. There is always a spiritual solution, whether it is a change in our perception or an actual change in conditions.

Revealed truth is alive. Only a higher Power could have inspired those words in James two thousand years ago and brought them to life for me that moment. "Every good gift" was not enough, for it continues: "and every *perfect* gift." Perfection is found only in Spirit. We experience it in deep meditation and spontaneous moments. We feel it in the purity of a child's love, when strangers risk their lives for others, and when a spiritual Presence is felt in nature, music, and art. It can be felt in a relationship, a cherished pet, a brief encounter. Nothing in the temporal world is perfect, yet spiritually there is nothing but perfection. We have to be alert to recognize the signs.

A Gift the World Cannot Give

Signs often come after the death of a loved one. Many have heard the deceased call out their names to ease their grief. They break through in dreams that communicate a specific message or fill us with love, not with the sorrow of separation. Some have discovered the person's favorite flower blooming where never planted or out of season, as if to say: "Be happy. I still am." Life is eternal, despite the ephemeral forms.

Shortly after her husband's death, my aunt was led to a book where she found a note he had written for her with instructions regarding a matter that troubled her after he died. His death was unexpected, and she had no reason to open that particular book at the time. The note resolved her dilemma and lifted her out of a black cloud of grief, for she felt his presence beside her as she read the message he had lovingly prepared in case he passed on before her.

Another woman I knew received a phone call from her only son shortly after his death, telling her where to find the key for a safe deposit box that held an important document for settling his affairs. Was it a dream or only a dream? She was a successful businessperson and did not think so. She knew nothing about his safe deposit box, and the key was exactly where he told her.

When meditation becomes a daily practice, veils thin between the temporal and the eternal, and a spiritual dimension can break through at any time. It often happens during meditation and just before falling asleep or waking when the ego is at rest. You know it is not coincidence or subconscious contents welling up in dreams when it leaves you bathed in love, clarifies a situation, or teaches you something you could not have known. It is a gift the world cannot give.

Intellectual analysis is important to elucidate us on many levels, but only spiritual discernment reveals the eternal. Those who are gifted with both levels of awareness are the world's great leaders, saints, artists, and innovators. Many who silently bless the world are unknown, but their legacies live on. Everything in the world eventually turns to dust, but goodness and truth remain forever in consciousness. As an inner Voice explained to me:

> Wealth is left at the grave,
> Fame lasts but a very short while,
> Time erases us all;
> Goodness remains in the ethers,
> Someone will catch it and smile.

The Nature of God as Spirit

James not only recognized the Source of every good and perfect gift, he also knew the nature of God as Spirit. His "Father of lights" sounds more like modern physics than religious dogma with its anthropomorphic God. The verse continues: "with whom there is no variableness, neither shadow of turning." If there is variableness or duplicity in a person or situation, it is not a perfect gift from above.

The signs are always there, but we ignore them. What seems good to the intellect is based on conditioning, desire, and limited knowledge, not on Omniscience. Omniscience is a facet of Spirit within everyone that knows the past, present and future in each moment and expresses as the highest good. Ask to see as Spirit sees. It is rarely what we think. Then watch Grace function in simple matters, as well as complex issues that may involve others near and far. This was not only true two- and three-thousand years ago: God is now as God was then. Grace flows fully in the present moment, but we have to be spiritually alert to receive it.

The truth revealed in James 1:17 came through in different words to a close friend who passed into her own light 30 years ago. One summer evening she looked out her windows above a city park and saw couples walking along the path on their way to a performance. As she watched them strolling hand-in-hand, she was overcome with longing for her husband who died a few years earlier. It was like watching a romantic movie in which she had been the star, only to be reminded she no longer had a part in the film.

Suddenly an inner Voice spoke: *"For every human good, there is a human evil."* Instantly the piercing agony she felt after her husband's death returned, and she was engulfed in grief. The gentle Voice continued, *"Spiritual good has no opposite,"* and instantaneously both her anguish and her longing vanished. She called me right after it happened with laughter and astonishment in her voice. Both emotional extremes disappeared in the awareness of a Presence that restored her spiritual balance and transported her into a dimension where I trust she is now.

It is an example that spiritual healing does not take time, but is the awareness of a higher Power in the moment. It reveals a peace not dependent on human good, dissolves pain and stress, and alters outer conditions. It does not mean the physical body will live forever or for many years. Casting off the shell that has fulfilled its purpose is the natural progression of the Soul en route to greater attainments. We cannot help feeling a loss when loved ones pass on, but if we realize the Source that brought them into our lives, spiritual connections continue and new roles unfold on both sides of the veil.

As the Voice said to my friend that summer night: "Spiritual good has no opposite," or as James expressed it: "no variableness, neither shadow of turning." Love would be a universal experience if everyone realized the "Father of lights" where every good and perfect gift originates.

Setting the Wheels in Motion

Every action we take in recognition of the same One in all sets the wheels of Grace in motion. We may have to begin with seemingly insignificant acts, but we must begin because the spiritual door opens only as we step forward with actions that express universal love. "God is love" is not a cliché. Everyone who has experienced the Divine in any era or tradition has felt an indescribable love.

We all share the same function: to release more

love than we came in with and ultimately rise into Love Itself. How to release more love depends on an individual's receptivity, aptitudes, and opportunities. We cannot be more than Spirit's expression as us, but we do not want to be less. The greater work is done in silence when we touch the Soul realm and Grace is released. Grace is invisible, but Its influence is omnipotent. In deep meditation the world disappears and the personal sense of self with it. We feel renewed because our real Self is untouched by temporal conditions, and the world is elevated because Grace has entered its atmosphere.

Be still and listen. If a word, phrase, or melody floats into your mind, or a sudden feeling of peace or uneasiness descends, pay attention. Be still and watch. Be willing to see what is revealed and witness Grace appearing in amazing ways. Be still and know *I* am that *I AM,* an inseparable, inaudible Presence that is always speaking and revealing Its love. There is no greater gift.

6

Resting in Spirit

*Thou wilt keep him in perfect peace
whose mind is stayed on thee.*

Isaiah, 800 BC

Imagine what it feels like to experience perfect peace, a peace that floods every cell of your body and stills every thought. Imagine a state of being without anger, fear, desire or regret. Isaiah experienced it. So did Jesus, Buddha, and other illumined beings. Imagination can serve as the first step on a bridge to take you there.

Nothing in the world promises perfect peace, yet ancient Hindu, Hebrew, Chinese, Greek, Buddhist, Christian, and many native traditions describe a dimension of oneness and peace beyond the physical world. It was not philosophy, theology, or myth to those whose records have survived; they experienced it. So do many people today. So can you.

A Different Approach

How do we keep the mind "stayed on thee," a dimension beyond the mind? Only in the depths of meditation or spontaneous awakenings does the mind become aware of a dimension beyond itself. Many think meditation is too difficult or takes too much time. They give up without trying and live on surfaces. Meditation is easy if you take a different approach. Rather than sit in an uncomfortable position and strive to reach a state of consciousness that is elusive, esoteric, or unknown, think of it as a rest from thoughts and things. A mind at rest is the natural state of being.

You drop everything when you rest. You do not rest to achieve something. Meditation on the spiritual path requires an additional step. As you close your eyes, make the conscious decision to open yourself to Soul, Spirit, or absolute Truth, and to *nothing else*. Eventually a mind that is one with the allness of Spirit can become as natural as breathing because spiritually there is only one Mind.

When you first enter the rest in meditation, it is important to focus the mind on an eternal truth, scriptural quotation, sacred word, or mantra, because to sit with a blank mind opens it to anything. As the mind wanders, return to your spiritual word or truth and ponder its meaning in quietness and alertness, receptive to what the Soul may impart. Watching the breath in meditation is another ancient practice that quiets thought and puts the ego in abeyance. Breathing changes. At the deeper stages, it slows down and seems to almost come to a stop. You do nothing to make it happen. You do not breathe for a purpose or try to slow your breathing; you just witness the changes that occur.

Spiritual stillness is alive; it is not a dead silence. The more you rest in the Spirit at the center of your being, the more you become aware of Its influence. Omniscience not only knows the best outcome in every situation, but is also the power to make it happen. Why would you want to be limited to your own ideas and efforts when Omniscience and Omnipotence are closer than breathing?

Only Grace assures the continuity of good. The loving support of others helps us survive life's challenges, but even the deepest love cannot heal someone's grief over the death of a loved one or alleviate distress and disease. A temporary remedy can alleviate pain but does not constitute health. Temporary peace is better than war, but is not lasting. Unless we experience the peace that releases Grace into the scene, we will not eradicate suffering or prevent the occurrence or re-occurrence of evils.

Anyone can dedicate at least 20 of 1440 minutes in a day to meditate. Start with five minutes after waking in the morning, before or after meals, and before bedtime.

Take several pauses throughout the day to consciously connect with a Presence that has an infinite reach. What begins with a few minutes of inner communion becomes longer and more frequent as the rhythm of Soul takes over. It is possible to cultivate a state of inner alertness wherever you are, not just in meditation, as if listening to the sounds of a secret garden growing. Expect to be amazed.

The Currents of Grace

Everyone yearns for fulfillment because it is the natural expression of an infinite Source. Many never realize their potential because they cling to ego desires and attachments, rather than open themselves to the currents of Grace. To live without desire does not mean to live without motivation, purpose, or love. The Soul always aspires to express Its fullness, and love is Its nature. Where these qualities are blocked, conflicts arise in the mind, body, and world.

People pray for peace as if an outside God has the power to give or withhold it. Peace, like love, is already established deep within everyone where it must be realized before it can come into expression. No one said it would be easy, but that "with God all things are possible."[1] What things? Only those that are supported by Grace. What is currently popular often leaves no lasting legacy, for Grace does not support the ego's accomplishments or perpetuate its failures.

As Spirit becomes more real to us than matter, our awareness of Grace expands. We have to be willing to act on the opportunities that present outwardly, and inwardly too. Eventually the problems of others come to our attention to be brought under Grace, for we no longer give them credence and Spirit knows no obstacles unto Itself. We may awaken in the night with a call for help on the spiritual plane from someone who may or may not be identified, or sense an impending danger that is thwarted if we go into meditation, realizing only one Presence and Power. When we reach a point of perfect peace or a spiritual truth is revealed within us, our work is done for the moment. There is no better place to go than the center of our own being where we touch the currents of Grace.

The Recognition that Blesses

When we rest in the peace of Soul, Grace is diffused like a delicate fragrance. An invisible aura spreads. It makes no difference if it emanates from someone in a church, temple, mosque, or ashram; alone in a desert; working in an international office; or serving coffee in a small cafe. Those who silently recognize a divine spark in others offer more than a service or hot beverage. Although the persons recognized have no understanding of what is happening, most will feel an uplift or peace.

When I was a child, my mother took me with her to a women's department store where I felt a unique sensation. I loved to go there because peace would flow through me whenever a soft-spoken saleswoman would speak to us, or a white-gloved elevator operator quietly ask what floor we wanted. I tingled from head to toe and intuitively knew if I spoke of it, the tingling would stop. After I felt the same sensation in meditation and as a sign when something is spiritually *real,* I realized the store's staff must have been trained to recognize the best in those they served.

Recognizing the Spirit in those we encounter changes lives, especially our own. It is not merely a subjective experience, for one person's silent awareness touches the Soul in others. It is specific as it affects the individuals and situations included in our realization of Oneness, unless minds and hearts are closed. That has nothing to do with us. Our part is to be an inlet and an outlet for Grace wherever we are.

"Know thyself" was important enough to the ancient Greeks to inscribe on a temple. When we realize the true nature of the Self, we discover we are one with the allness of Spirit and the allness of Spirit in each other. Since Omnipresence has no boundaries, we realize we are never confined to a physical body, circumstance, or place. If you feel limited, as everyone does in one way or another, try to put a wall around the Infinite. Think about this until you realize the infinite nature of your own being, for the truth removes all doubt.

An Inner Shift

Humanly we seem to live in our bodies, but we actually live in our minds. It takes an inner shift to live in the Spirit. The shift occurs in deep states of meditation when we feel something open or shift within us. Every shift in awareness brings a change in mind, body, behavior, or circumstance because all is consciousness expressing as form and idea.

The changes can be major or subtle. You feel lighter, freer, and fuller for no outer reason. Sometimes an invisible bubble pops that you did not know was there until it is gone. A weight falls off your shoulders; fear, conflicts or symptoms dissolve or diminish. Problems vanish or cease to disturb you. Solutions appear spontaneously or are unnecessary because you see the situation differently. Resting in Spirit is like physical exercise. It awakens our spiritual "muscles" as we rest from thinking and doing, from thinking of all we think we should be doing.

Take a few minutes and try it. Turn off the phone, the music, the TV, and close the door. Close the door to the mind too. Forget your worries, plans, hopes, and desires for the next few minutes. Drop your beliefs in or against a Supreme Being too, for they are your concepts, not God Itself. Let Truth reveal Itself. When personal or world thoughts barge in, do not let the mind run away with you. Unwanted thoughts "come to pass," unless we dwell on them. We know we are not the mind because we can decide what to focus the mind upon. A mind full of its own ideas is not an invitation for Spirit to enter or an entry point for Grace.

Be willing to rest in the silence for a few minutes or longer, and watch as an inner shift occurs. If you cannot take a few minutes each day to abide in your Soul, it shows how entangled in the ego you have become. The world will not come to an end if you are out of touch for a few minutes. As meditation becomes a regular practice, Grace becomes a continuing experience. No one can tell you what will happen or what you need to know. If you are persistent in your spiritual practice and patient in a flow that cannot be rushed, things occur that you could not have brought about or did not recognize before. Whatever is needed for your good will be revealed on the inner plane, or circumstances will naturally occur as evidence of Grace in your life. You are remembering your oneness in the Infinite Whole where Grace supports everything.

Perfect peace. Other goals pale in comparison. A moment of Grace clarifies thought and is the catalyst for harmony, wholeness, and healing. After many years of meditation and the conscious practice of spiritual principles, we discover we no longer need to meditate for long periods because we find ourselves living in a spiritual milieu. As you make meditation and spiritual principles a daily practice, you will have your own proofs of a higher Wisdom and Love, for there is no place where Spirit ends and a material world begins.

7

100 Percent Spirit

There is not a material body and a spiritual body.... Here, as in every aspect of life, the principle of oneness applies.[1]

Joel S. Goldsmith

One of the greatest fictions accepted as real is the belief in a soul separate from body or Spirit separate from matter as two distinct realities, rather than One Essence expressing as all. Ancient Eastern teachings acknowledge an apparent self and a spiritual Self, but only the latter is accepted as real. Jesus went further and revealed the spiritual nature of body. Rather than denying, denigrating, or renouncing the physical body, his awareness of 100 percent Spirit brought the spiritual body into manifestation.

The world was not ready for his perception, though some caught it through the centuries. Truth has never stopped revealing Itself, but only where

Spirit is realized as the only *reality* do spiritual laws function in our lives. The belief we are physical beings is an impassable barrier until we awaken to the omnipresence of Spirit.

No Gaps in Omnipresence

There are no gaps in Omnipresence where a physical universe could have come into existence. Despite how it looks or feels, the real body is incorporeal, ageless, and eternal; it cannot be reduced to a composition of cells or DNA. It is the body you have now and forever, but not the physical *sense* of body that is always changing and can be felt, weighed, and seen in a mirror. The truth does nothing for us unless we gain the realization ourselves.

The physical sense of body changes and dies, but the spiritual body exists forever at the standpoint of perfection. It is the basis of spiritual healing, which is actually the revealing of spiritual perfection appearing as form, character, activity, and truth. Nothing changes the perfection of being, but we can forget and behave in ways that are incongruent with our true Self. The more we acknowledge Spirit as the only reality, substance and law, the more It governs our lives, even in such practical things as the flow of traffic and the expansion of personal time. Jesus was not the only person who proved spiritual laws, but most could not bridge the gap between the allness of Spirit and a physical universe.

While there are no gaps in Omnipresence, there seem to be huge gaps in us.

In true meditation, i.e., without words, music or any outside stimuli, there is a point where we experience a dimension of perfect peace. Anxiety, conflicts, and symptoms diminish or dissolve, or there is a feeling of boundless bliss despite negative conditions or impending death. This is not only recorded in ancient Scriptures and myth, those dedicated to spiritual paths today witness evidence of Grace as an ongoing occurrence. Conscious oneness with God is the secret of harmony in every area of life, but we have forgotten the nature of God and ourselves as 100 percent Spirit.

There is no greater blessing than to realize your oneness with God. If your concept of "God" is too laden with anthropomorphic or negative images, realize oneness with your innermost being, Soul, or Spirit. It does not care what name you give It, because the reality is beyond words and thoughts. Close your eyes and feel the reality of your own being. It exists beneath your thoughts and emotions and includes your real body. At first it may seem that the mind will never calm down, but the mind is not your eternal identity. Ignore it in the realization of the Self that can choose to ignore it. Be still and listen as Truth utters Itself within you:

There is no place where
Spirit ends and I begin:
I in Thee and Thou in Me,
Indivisibly, eternally
One

The Efficacy of Grace

After we have witnessed symptoms, danger, lack, storms, and discords dissolve or diminish for decades when seeking only the awareness of Spirit or Omnipresence, we never again doubt the efficacy of Grace. If everyone acknowledged Spirit as the only reality, peace would naturally follow, and there would be no battlefields in the world, the mind, or the body. An improved sense of health is only one of the effects.

Those who are spiritually awake have far less need of medical remedies. When confronted with an appearance of illness or injury, they seek first an adjustment in consciousness. Why some healings are quick and others take time or never seem to happen, we do not know. We do not know what needs to be healed in others or ourselves. Life is not as it seems. There is an immense gap between spiritual awareness and intellectual knowledge. The gap begins to close with the recognition of 100 percent Spirit.

The temporal world is part of a vast universal illusion or misperception. You are *real,* creation is *real,* but the perception of material roses in a material garden is as illusory as monsters under the bed, the physical body as illusory as its symptoms. Seen through the ego, everything is transitory and imperfect; seen through spiritual discernment there is only the eternality of infinite perfection. The spiritual rose never dies and includes within itself the rosebud and the rose in full bloom, as well as in its dormant periods. The same is true of the Self.

The Canal of Individual Awareness

Years ago I was shown in a flash how individual consciousness expresses. I saw the image of a ship going through a canal. As water filled the lock, the ship rose to the top, but other ships remained stuck at lower levels. Then an inner Voice said: *"There is fulfillment for every level of consciousness."* I saw that Grace is available at every stage of life, but only when we are willing to release our attachments do circumstances appear that raise us to a higher level. The boundaries are self-imposed, although it may not seem to be so.

Recently I saw someone spontaneously healed of a long-standing ailment after she asked for spiritual help, yet not for a second did she realize she may have avoided surgery for another condition. It does not mean that surgery can always be avoided, but not to be mentally bound by anything but Spirit. Then if surgery is necessary, it goes well and the recovery is easier than expected. Or if it is time to depart, we go in peace, ready—sometimes eager—for the next experience to begin.

Since Spirit fills all space, why do discords, illnesses, pains, and limitations linger where there is spiritual realization? Grace is available at every level of awareness but functions within the parameters we set, like the ships I was shown inside a canal. There are degrees of realization and barriers we do not see. Sometimes the realization is not deep enough to dissolve the problem. Some universal beliefs are so strong, they seem indissoluble, or the experience may be part of a refining process. Our part is not to judge, but to acknowledge Spirit in all our ways.

We have forgotten our real existence as Spirit. The result is noise rather than melody, harshness rather than lullaby. When we realize we are one with the Essence of everyone, the right melodies play by themselves. Sometimes the breaking up of current situations is necessary for spiritual fulfillment to manifest. Only those who are awake recognize what is happening.

A friend described an illumined teacher as looking "terrible" after a heart attack. A more enlightened person said: "He was living in the resurrection." His commitment and stamina never wavered, and he was able to complete his work before he passed on peacefully a few years later. The first saw through physical eyes a weak and diminished body; the second saw through spiritual discernment the magnitude of Soul shining through an almost transparent physical form. Spiritual being, like beauty, is in the awareness of the beholder. As Omnipresence becomes more real to us than the physical world, the truth behind appearances becomes more apparent. The gap is smaller within us.

A Receiving Station for Spirit

In meditation the function of the mind changes. It becomes a receiving station for Spirit, rather than a sponge for human theories, statistics, and beliefs. Mystics of East and West have left records revealing a higher Power and dimension, yet many remained under a belief in duality. They accepted the belief in a life, body, world, and spirits apart from God, rather than the realization of one Presence, Power, and Life.

Where the allness of Spirit is accepted, it is reflected in a person's experience. You can easily test yourself on this. Begin to recognize God or Spirit as the only Substance, Cause, Law and Effect when confronted with discords, disasters, limitation, and disease. It will not bring everyone or everything into harmony, but if you accept negative conditions as real or inevitable, that is certain to be your experience and susceptibility.

The Light shines brightest on those who stand naked beneath Its rays, without the layers of false beliefs, ego defenses, and material desires. No one can promise illumination to another, but it can be sparked by those whose light outshines the darkness in us. The awareness will not last if we do not find it within ourselves. Everyone receives it from the same Source. When we are receptive to the spiritual impulse, Grace impels us to our highest good and reveals those attuned to the same frequency. It makes no difference whether they live in the same city, across the ocean, or in other dimensions.

Beyond Explanation

Sometimes it takes a brush with death to awaken us. A young woman I met in Florida was driving home on a dark night in a torrential rainstorm on I-95 where the traffic never ceases. Suddenly a huge green truck was about to run her car into the concrete barrier. She had no time to react and felt her car "lifted up" over the highway. Still shaking when she got home, she noticed green paint where the truck had struck the side of her car. There is no physical explanation why there had not been a major collision. She is certain that angels lifted her car above the road and saved her life.

Not long ago a friend visited Vancouver for the first time. While looking for the street to return her small rental car, she was distracted. When she saw the right street sign, she turned without looking both ways. Suddenly she caught sight of a cable-bus entering the same lane from an intersecting street. As she heard the loud screech of brakes, she knew she would be crushed. The next moment she saw the bus continuing on its way. It was impossible. She too felt an angel prevented her death.

I had a similar experience years ago when a red semi-truck suddenly appeared in my rearview mirror going full speed inches behind my car. There was no way my compact car could go fast enough to get out of its way and nowhere to turn during rush hour on a city highway. I knew I would be severely injured or killed, leaving my young sons without a mother. Suddenly the truck was nowhere in sight, although there were no nearby exits. I was still shaking when I arrived at my destination. It happened in an instant as these things always do. I had no doubt a higher Power saved my life.

Whether attributed to angels, God, a higher Power or Grace, it is a Presence that overcomes material laws because there are none to be overcome *in Spirit.* The above incidents are typical of many that confirm we do not die until our time has come. While most of us do not know how long we will be here, we do not have to accept accidents, disasters, or disease as inevitable, for they are not spiritually maintained. The same Power that can change physical circumstances on the highway can also change the physical body. Why? *Because reality is spiritual, not physical.* Our experience depends on what we accept as real in our awareness.

8

A New Dawn

Dark is the world to thee: thyself art the reason why;
For is He not all but thou, that hast power to feel
'I am I'?

Alfred, Lord Tennyson, 1877

No matter how dark life seems at times, a new dawn is always present behind the horizons in our lives. It is as certain as the morning sun to appear if we realize our true identity. Dark nights occur only in the mind that has forgotten *I am I*. When Spirit dawns in our awareness, we realize we are one with an infinitely loving Presence that never leaves us, despite our failings or denials.

Living with only a mental or physical sense of self always brings dark nights. At times it feels like walking with blinders along a cliff, or falling on sharp rocks, or into deep chasms with no way out. All the while a loving Hand is guiding us beside still waters. The still waters of Spirit are not just a state of mind, but an invisible current that floats us to ever-expanding horizons. Dark nights occur in the mind; the Soul is always in God's keeping.

When Spirit Dawns

When dawn comes each morning, we take it for granted. We have forgotten the magnificence of daybreak. Out of the dark a blazing light lifts its golden crest above the horizon like magic. A huge glowing ball slowly rises into the sky, illuminating a shadowy earth that comes into focus in living color. Strange, ominous shapes formerly engulfed in darkness become warm and familiar in the dawn's early light. There is nothing like the first light of the day. We know it is not magic but the natural order of the earth orbiting the sun.

Grace is the natural orbit of Soul ordering our lives. Even when we seem engulfed in mental, emotional, physical, or financial darkness, Grace is present behind the darkness, waiting to release Its rays into our lives. When Spirit dawns in our awareness, life takes on a glow that changes everything. Even if nothing outwardly changes, life looks different in the light.

The darkness in life seems real. Death seems real, yet no one has ever ceased to exist. The physical body is not and never was the real person. It is an instrument for the one who temporarily occupies it. We pass onwards, we do not end, as everyone who has had a near-death experience knows. Eventually we realize *I am I,* inseparable from the Source that brought us into being. It is a mystery and a paradox: to be wholly one with a Presence that is wholly one with us, yet is infinitely more than any single expression. To read "I am I" does nothing. To hear *I am I* spoken by a still, small Voice within you reveals the mystical *I* that is your real Self and the real Self of everyone.

The same awareness has been described by illumined masters, saints, poets, artists, composers, writers, and countless anonymous people living dedicated lives. While few have attained full illumination, all lose their fear of death. Their words point the way to a dimension that only becomes real for us by experience. They also let us know we are in good company.

Healing on the Mystical Level

As spiritual masters have known since ancient times and physicists have discovered in modern times, there are invisible connections that operate beyond our comprehension. We seem to live separate lives in a physical world when we are actually living in a spiritual universe where everything is connected. It explains how healing happens when we reach out for help or prayer from someone who is spiritually awake.

Healing on the mystical level is not the result of

gaining God's favor, blind faith, positive thinking, or mind over matter. Healing is the revealing of Omnipresence when the nature of spiritual reality is realized by an individual *now*. Yesterday's realization does not help anyone today. Spiritual healing, harmony or wholeness appears when an inner release is felt, or a dimension of perfect peace lifts us out of ourselves, or words of truth are heard as confirmation that Spirit is on the scene.

Spiritual healing or harmony has nothing to do with the gravity of personal or world conditions, but with clearing our inner vision in the realization of an eternal spiritual dimension or "kingdom" where only perfection is. It does not mean that everything will be fine in the three-dimensional world, for we do not know what has to occur for individuals and the world to awaken, but our inner work is done when the release is felt.

Sometimes the darkness in life seems so real, we need the help of a more spiritually enlightened person to break through whatever seems to be binding or harming us or persons we hold dear. Those who have a healing consciousness know there is only one Presence and Power, despite what is appearing in the human scene. Even an instant of spiritual realization can bring an inner release, healing, or solution, or the dissolution of adverse conditions. All spiritual healing is instantaneous, although it can take hours, days, months, or even years for the completed demonstration to appear.

As the physical sense of life breaks in the mind of the person or "practitioner" called upon for prayer, a release is felt in the mind, body, or circumstances of the persons who ask for help because they have attuned to the same Spirit within themselves. Grace is released into the situation because we live in a spiritual universe where everything is connected. Spiritual connections also occur when two or more persons are moved by the same impulse at the same time. They may not know the other exists or that they share a mutual purpose until they meet. Grace usually appears in natural ways, but anything can happen when we realize our oneness with the Infinite Whole.

Entertaining Angels

A man in touch with me answered his door this week to a neighbor and her companion. When they realized they had awakened him from a nap, they did not want to disturb him and left. Later he asked his neighbor about her friend, for she had made a deep impression on him. His neighbor said no one was with her, but she too had felt a loving presence.

The woman he saw standing at the door behind his neighbor felt as loving as his mother. Not only did he feel her love, he was astonished when he learned his neighbor had come alone. The experience helped to ease his grief later that day when he learned one of his closest friends died unexpectedly in a distant city. Despite the dark clouds in his life at the time, the woman he saw standing behind his neighbor was proof he was not facing them alone.

At the time this college professor was making an effort to realize his oneness with God in the midst of hostile circumstances. He had lost his teaching position through no fault of his own and was living far from friends and family. As he was working as a night watchman to pay for necessities, something more was happening on the inner plane. Within a few years he found a fulfilling new love and life in a place he had never imagined while living in a remote college town where he felt no spiritual welcome.

"Be not forgetful to entertain strangers: for thereby some have entertained angels unaware."[1] It happens more often than we recognize when someone comes into our lives to fill an urgent need or teach us something we need to know. Usually it happens in natural ways, but many have had experiences when a person suddenly appears as help or reassurance—often in a life-threatening situation—and then vanishes.

When we consciously surrender to the Spirit in the midst of us, amazing things happen. Sometimes Grace appears in incredible ways, like the messenger of love who appeared at my friend's door, sometimes as simple acts of kindness, always as reassurance.

Spiritual Readiness

Divine love is never frightening. It is only the ego that fears its demise. Many stories have been told about the temptations that come to those who undergo spiritual initiation. If they failed the tests, usually because of fear for their lives or the lives of loved ones, they were thrown out of spiritual brotherhoods because they were incapable of the deeper experiences. Good intentions have nothing to do with spiritual readiness.

Spiritual readiness comes by Grace and is the surrender of the ego with its fears, desires, judgments, pride, and false sense of unworthiness. Humility is not to degrade the Self that is one of God's infinite expressions; rather, it is the recognition that the ego cannot take credit for good. We do not always recognize our weaknesses nor can we overcome them by good intentions, but we can be willing to release them. It only takes our willingness for Grace to operate.

No illumined persons claim to be good or to have supernatural powers of themselves. Neither Jesus, nor Buddha, nor any of the saints, nor Old Testament leaders made such claims. Like us, they could only be witnesses to an invisible Presence and Power. Unlike us, they were so aware of the Eternal that they did not waver when faced with temptation, danger, or death. When Jesus said, "I have overcome the world,"[2] he did not mean the Sanhedrin, Roman leaders, soldiers, human cruelty or injustice: he had overcome the temporal sense of world within himself.

Purity of intent leads to the door, but it opens by Grace. Whenever we know the truth about anything, false information no longer binds us. We still see a horizon in the distance, but no longer fear to fall off the earth's edge. Those who are spiritually awake still see physical bodies and a physical world, but know better than to accept the outer forms as the *reality*. This is not a denial of the need for improvement or "redemption" on the human plane, but the recognition that the real need is to spiritually awaken. The Redeemer is the mystical *I* that indwells everyone. Illumined beings stand by to help anyone who reaches out to them, but spiritual readiness comes by Grace.

No Interference in Oneness

I am I is not a connection to a Deity or Power outside of ourselves, but realizing that which *is* and has always been our true nature. The earth and the sun are 93 million miles apart, yet the earth is held in its orbit by the gravity pull of the sun. Nothing interferes, not the distance of time or space, or the many celestial bodies and "space junk" in between. Just as nothing interferes with the earth's orbit, nothing can interfere with the Soul's orbit if we go within where it functions.

Although God may seem 93 million miles away or not exist, we only seem cut off from God because of the junk beliefs we have accepted about the nature of God and ourselves. We have forgotten the Creative Principle that formed us out of Itself and maintains us in our rightful orbits. We have forgotten that we did not begin at birth and do not end at death. We have forgotten our oneness with the Essence that is everyone's true nature.

The world would soon change if all children were taught to silently recognize the same Spirit in all. There is no better legacy to give our children than the revelation that the Source of all good is within themselves and is equally present in everyone. Our silent recognition of the same One in all dissolves the sense of separation from God and each other. Silence gives the ego no credit and does not encounter interference or resistance. That is why silence and secrecy will always be part of the spiritual life.

All spiritual experiences happen in the Soul, even if a vision seems to appear outwardly. I know a young man who never doubts his eternality after seeing a Light "brighter than the sun" when he was in high school. Yet his brother asleep in the same room was not awakened by it. We may never see a light, but when we open ourselves unconditionally to the Source of our being, It radiates into our lives. A vast reservoir of love begins operating in us, for us, and through us.

It is no more possible to realize your oneness with Spirit and remain separate from Grace than to stand naked in the sun and hide from its rays. The radiance is always there, closer than breathing, when the realization of *I am I* returns. As Tennyson continues in "The Higher Pantheism":

> *Speak to Him, thou, for He hears,*
> *and Spirit with Spirit can meet–*
> *Closer is He than breathing,*
> *and nearer than hands and feet.*

9

Our Spiritual Orbit

*All that is part of your fulfillment is held
in the invisible circle of your own consciousness.*

An Inner Voice

Once we experience our oneness with God, the world loses its attraction. We are no longer enticed by what most people desire, except for those parts that touch our spiritual frequency. We go through transitions that happen to everyone, with one foot established in Spirit and the other stuck in the world's illusions of "I need, I want, I must," as the earthly pull lessens.

We know what is happening, but we are still entrapped in the dream. Perhaps it never wholly dissolves as long as we exist on earth, but it no longer grips us as deeply or fools us as long after we have realized the spiritual nature of reality and our self-completeness in Spirit.

The Circle of Self-Completeness

Self-completeness is like a circle. All that is part of your fulfillment is held in the invisible circle of your own consciousness. You never have to go outside that circle. It is a world unto you, the world that has been prepared for you from the beginning. You recognize those in your circle by the double delight that is felt: each for each. The "circle" is the Consciousness or Soul of the individual, not the rational mind or brain.

We all have an invisible circle that holds our good in trust. Rest in the awareness that your good is already established in that circle. The more you rest in the completeness of your own Consciousness, the more its harmonies appear as persons, places, activities, circumstances, and things that are qualities of Self-completeness in outer expression.

Our part is to go within and *let* our good appear, as we fulfill our daily responsibilities. Everything is included in that invisible circle and held in trust for us, a divine trust that cannot be broken or infringed upon. What was established as ours from the beginning, no one can touch. It is only the ego that makes the wrong choices.

Later that circle was revealed as a spiritual orbit that holds all that is meant for us in perfect rhythm, and the words came: *Stay in your own orbit.* The constellations appear in the right time and order if we are true to our innermost Self, which is one with all spiritual creation and governed by Grace. Those who meditate discover their own frequency, an individual rhythm that is experienced in deep states of meditation. That rhythm is our link with the whole spiritual universe because Spirit is inseparable from Its expressions, with which we are indivisibly and eternally One.

The Whole Ocean

Just as the whole ocean supports each wave, the allness of Spirit supports each of Its individual expressions. This is not true about the human personality that was born, ages, dies, and is subject to chance, ignorance, disease, lack, and karma or the law of cause and effect, which operates until we come under Grace.

We can never know the truth about ourselves or others by mental or physical analysis; we have to return to the Source. While the properties of seawater can be found in a single drop, examining a drop by itself would never reveal the magnitude of ocean or a vial of air the cosmos. Without a glimpse of the greater whole, the depths, heights, immensity, might, mysteries, and majesty of ocean would remain unknown. When the same drop is thrown back into the sea, it becomes an inseparable part of the ocean.

When we realize we are inseparable from the Source of all that is real and eternal, we become an essential part of the Infinite Whole. We find ourselves and all that is meant for us moved like waves by the propulsion of an invisible Presence. A wave does not have to figure out where it is going, nor could it get there on its own. Living by Grace does not mean to do nothing; it means to be willing to yield to a spiritual impulse. We make plans as a natural part of life, but have to be willing to change them at a moment's notice in response to a spiritual urge. Our plans may have nothing to do with the divine plan.

The best plan is take time each day to rest like a wave in an infinite sea and let ourselves be moved by an indwelling Presence that includes all within Itself. Then as the days, months, and years pass, we find all that is part of our completeness propelled by the same invisible current. Remind yourself often in the silence of your own being:

The allness of Spirit—
the whole spiritual universe—
supports me in the recognition
that "I and my Father" are indivisibly
and eternally One. I know not Its plan,
but I can rest in the awareness of oneness
with the whole "Ocean" of God and
watch the **I** that **I AM**
fulfilling Itself in ways beyond
imagination, reason, and personal efforts.

"All that the Father giveth me shall come to me"[1] applies to everyone. Jesus was teaching universal laws that operate when we realize our oneness with the Father he said is equally ours. It is a movement in Spirit that manifests when we realize our self-completeness in Soul where Grace functions.

Soul Constellations

Although many accept the concept of "soul" on religious or philosophical grounds, few are aware of the Soul realm in themselves. Unless we realize Soul as our real identity, we are vulnerable to every statistic, condition, and belief. In deep states of meditation, we touch pure Consciousness, vulnerable only to spiritual law. The weight of mind and body dissolves in the buoyancy of Spirit where Grace functions and the Soul's constellations occur.

There is nothing missing or amiss in the completeness of Spirit or Its individual expressions. What seems absent may be waiting for our attunement on the inner plane or the right timing. We cannot hurry the process anymore than we can hurry the sun, but just as we can block the sun from shining through our windows, we can remove ourselves from Grace. To think we are solely responsible for maintaining ourselves cuts off the whole "Ocean" that is there to support Its expression as us.

When we realize we are one with all spiritual creation and stay centered in our own orbit, letting nothing disturb the peace of Soul in ourselves, Grace takes over and directs the timing, the scenes, and the players. There is a point of stillness reached in meditation that governs the synchronicity of outer events. Just as the stars and planets appear in their right constellations, the right circumstances, persons, and activities appear at the right time. We cannot "do" anything to make it happen.

More important than anything we are doing is to be spiritually awake while doing it. After his enlightenment Buddha was asked if he were a god. No, he replied. Are you an angel? No. Then what are you? I am awake, he said. We too must be awake, or we miss the significance of the moment and shut the door to the Grace that is always present. After a deep meditation we may feel a burst of energy and initiate or accomplish things previously blocked or never considered. Or we may be pulled into such a deep inner space that we want only to rest in the bliss of spiritual communion until the feeling passes. What looks like doing nothing may be the consummation of events that later appear.

Often the most significant moments in life have nothing to do with our plans, but happen along the way. Everything is already established in our spiritual orbits and appears in its rightful time and rhythm when we realize our self-completeness in and as Spirit. It may involve something that seems beyond our human capacities, but it is never a burden when it is our own constellations in motion.

Spiritual Affinities and Identities

There are connections in the invisible we are not aware of until they appear. Spiritual affinities operate on a deeper level than mental and physical attractions. Attractions are based on the desire for someone or something that seems appealing on the physical plane. They usually involve competition and often manipulation. Spiritual affinities reveal a oneness already established, though you may have just met. We know not in advance who or what is in our circle of being, but there is mutual recognition, never competition, where there is a spiritual connection. It may be unspoken, but the Soul always responds.

Circumstances change, for we cannot control the actions of others, but our good remains secure in our spiritual orbits. The strongest relationships are indestructible and undying. Some relationships remain on the inner plane and may or may not be revealed when meditation dissolves the belief in separation. Our experience depends on the self we identify with: the false ego based on a physical body, limited mind, and personal experience, or the Self that is one with Its Source.

Even in dormant periods, there is nothing missing

in anyone's spiritual identity. A tree does not always appear in full bloom, yet it is the same tree in winter when its branches are bare, as in summer when they are dense with foliage. The mature tree is the same tree that it was as a sapling, and you are the same spiritual identity that you were as a child with your constellations intact. You are the same *individual being* this moment that you were ten years, ten minutes and ten seconds ago. Your appearance changes, but not who and what you essentially and eternally are.

Do you think you will be any less or more *you* after the appearance called death? Or that you did not exist in some form and dimension before birth? Bodies change. Beliefs come and go. Spiritual identity is eternal; only the outer form changes. Everything is consummated within our own being, and the catalyst that brings it into expression is spiritual awareness.

Nothing Happens by Chance

Consciousness is the substance of all form. What seems random or uncertain is evidence of an indiscernible pattern based on immutable laws where nothing happens by chance. I was shown that seemingly random events are the result of prior events from a set of options that were self-determined by previous choices. Each choice or action generates invisible connections that only seem unrelated because we have forgotten what set them in motion.

The relationship between cause and effect is complex and subtle, hidden to all but the most discerning. Even the circumstances of birth are the result of former choices no longer remembered. There is no way to predict with certainty a future outcome since every subsequent choice creates another set of options that eventually appear as a present situation. Yet we always have the freedom to choose again from the options that seem to spontaneously occur. The patterns continue infinitely until the Infinite is allowed to take over. Regardless of how limited or extensive the options, realizing our oneness *with* and *in* Spirit breaks the patterns that result from previous choices or karma.

Chance has no place in God's plan. We either consciously dwell in oneness with an infinite Source, or as a separate sense of self that is vulnerable to good and evil, loss and gain, disease and health, and every form of duality. It is not mysterious, but we have forgotten the connection. The deeper our awareness of Spirit in meditation, the more we witness the effects, not only for ourselves but for others because of the principle of Oneness.

"That which is governing me is governing thee" is a truth to be realized for everyone in our experience and is the only way to come under Grace ourselves. The effects echo through time, for the gifts of the Spirit are never for one person alone. To love a child affects not only the child, but also everyone the child will affect in his or her lifetime. Those who die for freedom free future generations in which they too may return. Every realization of Oneness and unselfish act remain in consciousness to uplift, enfold, inspire, and free others.

As we stay in our own orbits, centered in the peace of Soul, and make meditation and spiritual principles a daily practice, we touch the dimension where our good is held in trust: *a divine trust that cannot be broken or infringed upon.* The boundaries of what begins as an invisible circle dissolve in the omnipresence of Grace.

10

The Power of Prayer

*God is a Spirit: and they that worship him
must worship him in spirit and in truth.*

John 4:24

There is no more powerful action than prayer,
so why do most prayers go unanswered? The truth
is that every prayer we could ever voice has already
been answered. The purpose of prayer is not to ask a
Supreme Being for anything but to align ourselves with
a spiritual Presence that has already given Its all.

Answered prayer is a Soul experience beyond words
and thoughts. Words are only the preparation. It is in
the depths of our being—*in Spirit and in Truth*—that
we enter the realm of answered prayer: a state of communion that is a catalyst for Grace. Each experience
strengthens our faith in a Presence that appearances
always deny.

Omnipresence Now

Answered prayer depends on what is more real in our awareness: Omnipresence or appearances, Spirit or matter. Few on earth think about Omnipresence, and fewer still ponder Its significance. Those who claim to believe in the religious concept contradict themselves if they accept a presence or power apart from God or a God who punishes. No true mystic has ever reported meeting such a God.

When we awaken to the nature of God as the omnipresence of love *now*, we begin to witness evidence all around us. Omnipresence realized always reveals a blessing, though it may not seem so in the moment. We do not see the invisible reality, and spiritual good has nothing to do with temporal values. Regardless of how astonishing the evidence, illumined masters warn not to rejoice in material demonstrations or psychic experiences; rather rejoice in our oneness with God. Oneness with God is true of everyone, although many fall far beneath their spiritual heritage. They will face their own consequences until they awaken, for cosmic laws are as exacting as electricity. What others do ultimately harms only themselves unless we accept a power apart from Spirit and set up a conflict within ourselves.

When we fail to acknowledge Omnipresence, we suffer from our own beliefs. It takes spiritual discernment to "see" the unseen. It does not mean to deny evil persons, actions, or conditions, but to drop both in the awareness of a spiritual Presence that is everywhere present, though invisible and forgotten. The reason most people are vulnerable to the same conditions is that they accept the same filters in the mind of a life, body, persons, and conditions apart from God, rather than an all-spiritual universe under Grace. We are all vulnerable until we establish spiritual truth in our awareness, and our vulnerability lessens. Then we witness evidence of a higher Power operating in human affairs.

The inner spark is lit by the intent of the heart, but we have to assert dominion over the mind with frequent reminders:

I respond only to God
and no longer allow the ego,
past circumstances, or outside
forces to influence me.
Awake or asleep, I rest in
the Spirit at the center of my being
and release those held
in my awareness to the same
Spirit within them.

A Higher Authority

The unawakened mind accepts whatever universal beliefs suggest, especially when it comes from someone considered an authority. Grace functions where a higher Authority than human is recognized. Many who dwell in spiritual awareness have enjoyed decades of health or a feeling of well-being despite medical predictions or physical limitations. Grace is dependent upon nothing, but the greater works appear only where Spirit has been realized in an individual's awareness.

Realization is a Soul experience. We are lifted into another dimension where we experience the peace of a spiritual Presence, regardless of what may be happening outwardly. Sometimes there are issues in consciousness that must be resolved before spiritual wholeness is felt or manifested. Some catch it while dying and enter the next dimension in a higher state of awareness. Being awake is important at every stage of existence.

The spiritual path has been called the "razor's edge" because an inner reprimand is felt whenever we violate the law of love. As we become more spiritually aware, the blade cuts more sharply. The "razor" sharpens us to recognize our mistakes, make the corrections within ourselves, and bring our outer behavior into spiritual alignment.

Miracles or Metaphors

People around the world are awakening to a deeper spirituality in themselves and to the same Spirit in all. When the experience is deep enough, miracles happen. A "miracle" is Grace breaking through in natural and supernatural ways, often where circumstances seem impossible.

Whether you believe miracles in the Bible were actual happenings or metaphors and allegories, inspired verses reveal eternal truths that are practical now. A literal or intellectual interpretation of Scripture may be interesting, fascinating, false or true, but does nothing now. When the hidden meaning of an inspired passage or a eternal truth is revealed within you, miracles happen. Thousands have seen their own "Red Seas" open in impossible situations, or Grace appear in tangible form to fill an urgent need, like the manna that fell in the desert to feed the Israelites. Eastern religions describe happenings no less amazing.

Grace operates beyond religious distinctions. Many have experienced changes in personality, body, or circumstances after they experienced a spiritual Presence or felt a robe of peace descend upon them in the midst of threatening or stressful situations. They may not have been believers before; afterwards they did not believe: they *knew*. Some of us have had near-death experiences and chose or were told to return. It has happened to enough people that we know it is not imagination, but even if it happened only to you, you *know* when it is real.

Spirit will never be seen through a telescope, under a microscope, captured in a test tube, or explained by a mathematical formula. It is the Essence behind the visible, the math, and the science, and can only be spiritually discerned. The real Self of you can only be spiritually discerned. It bears little resemblance to the physical form that changes from infancy to adulthood to old age to dust and then reforms anew. Consciousness never ceases.

In meditation an underlying stillness surfaces in the mind. Spiritual realization occurs when we are lifted into a dimension of perfect peace or an eternal truth is revealed within us. Even an instant of realization can dissolve grief, stop a storm or a heart attack, and reveal solutions. If a physical condition does not spiritually yield, Grace can appear as the right remedy, physician, or therapist. It brings harmony in relationships and peace in war if true peace, not supremacy, is sought.

Unlike cosmic laws and mental power, which can be used for good or for evil, Spirit cannot be used. It is what It IS eternally: an all-knowing Intelligence and all-embracing Love. How we identified with the image of a judgmental God and a selfhood apart from God shows how far we have wandered from the nature of God as Spirit and ourselves as Spirit individually expressed.

The Truth about Answered Prayer

Answered prayer is the awareness of that which eternally *IS*. When we are aware of the fragrance of flowers, it registers in the mind, but we did not beg, appease, attract, or affirm the flowers or the fragrance into being. Using pleas, sacrifice, or rituals in an attempt to influence God is not prayer, even if these techniques seem to work at times.

Prayer is not asking for something, as if Omnipresence were not always expressing Its fullness; prayer is a state of receptivity that we might be filled with that fullness. There is no "God" out there to persuade, no God who favors some and allows others to suffer; there is only *I*. Conscious oneness with God does not reveal anything outside of Itself: *There is nothing outside of Itself.*

Jesus often went apart from his disciples to pray, because the world is a constant denial of a Presence that is only and always love. We too need to "go apart" if we want to establish ourselves in Spirit. For the next 15 or 20 minutes, be still and let the peace of Soul permeate your being, your body, and your world, for they are contained in the Consciousness that you are. Rest in the I of your innermost being, and be still. Few are consciously attuned to what is only revealed in stillness.

Thoughts never reach the elevation of Spirit unless Spirit initiates the thought. Rather than use thoughts in an attempt to manifest a desire or plead with a mythical god to grant personal petitions, use your thoughts to open yourself to the Infinite. As the unity of Soul and Spirit dawns within us, doubt and anxiety dissolve in a divine assurance. It has nothing to do with beliefs.

Beliefs are of the mind; Oneness is of the Spirit. Ponder the Source and Substance of all that is now, has ever been, and will ever be, and discover your eternality. Then watch an underlying Presence bring all things together for good.

The Great Secret

Jesus revealed, "*I* am the way, the truth and the life,"[1] but his followers personalized the *I* unto Jesus and the great secret was lost. Perhaps no one has come close to the consciousness Jesus attained, but those who experience the Eternal discover the same mystical *I* and spiritual dimension, despite the diversity of descriptions. Once the *I* of your being reveals Itself, all arguments crumble into dust. Even the dust dissolves in the awareness of the *I* or Spirit that is everyone's true identity.

The mystery and the miracle is that wherever the nature of the Self is realized, we discover *I* at the core of our being includes the reality of all being. As the veils between "I and the Father" dissolve in meditation, we become more responsive to the spiritual impulse. We need to ask ourselves: What did Jesus experience? What did Buddha experience? What did the mystics and saints of the world experience? Only the Spirit within you can reveal the answer.

Even death cannot prevent the awareness of eternal life. Life's greatest sorrow for most people is the death of a loved one, yet no one dies on the spiritual plane and there is no lapse of consciousness while passing on. Upon learning of the sudden death of a spiritual teacher with whom I had been in close contact, I immediately went into meditation. The instant I closed my eyes, all sense of separation dissolved in what seemed her parting message that went far beyond the words: *"Nothing has ever happened but God."* Never believe death can prevent someone from reaching you if there is something important to impart.

The original purpose of meditation was to attain illumination or conscious oneness with God *now*. Oneness means absolute, complete union, not partial or occurring only after we die. The Hindu *Upanishads* state: "THOU ART THAT," not "THOU WILL BECOME THAT" in the future or after fulfilling certain rules or rituals. It does not refer to the ego or rational self, but to THAT which constitutes our real and eternal identity. Relax in an invisible Love that knows how to fulfill Itself as you and those in your awareness and is doing it now. Realization is what brings it into outer expression.

Many forms of meditation in the West are practiced for mental and physical well-being. It is a step in the right direction, but often remains a mental and physical exercise without spiritual awakening. If spiritual truth is not established in our awareness, material beliefs continue to operate in our experience. The slightest blip on our spiritual radar operates because there is no unexpressed consciousness. When meditation deepens, we feel an inner shift. If after several weeks or months you do not feel a shift in awareness, ask within to be shown your barriers. Sometimes we have to acknowledge our barriers to become conscious of the allness of Spirit and unblock the allness of Grace.

The power of prayer occurs in moments of inner communion when a spiritual Presence carries us and all that concerns us. It culminates in an experience of union where there is only *I*. These are not just mental experiences, for Grace is never confined to the mind. The deep well of peace that washes over us can accomplish in an instant what we of ourselves could not do in a lifetime. That is why it has been called "amazing Grace."

11

The Cloth Is Tightly Woven

The cloth is tightly woven,
the threads transparent.

An Inner Voice

Those who wear the robe of spiritual illumination know the cloth is tightly woven. The threads are
transparent to let in the light, but the weave is tight so
that neither the dirt nor the drivel of duality can get
through. Nothing unlike God takes root in the one
Mind that is the true mind of everyone. The cloth is
tightly woven, but the threads are pliable, repelling the
storms of material sense that never touch the peace of
Soul or enter Its kingdom.

When a strong wind scatters trash over a widespread
area, we see it with our eyes but not for a second do we
believe the debris is part of the natural landscape. The
mind that is awake does not wear a blindfold or bury its
brain in the sand. It does not deny individual and world

crises, but knows these are never part of the spiritual landscape. The awareness often dispels the shadows of physical sense and reveals a higher Power in the midst of us.

Evil Unmasked

As the veils between physical sense and spiritual reality dissolve, evils are unmasked in the realization that they have no spiritual law or power. Ancient truths come alive, and modern discoveries in physics reveal deeper implications. Physical phenomena can never reveal the Spirit behind the universe, but the implications are there for those who awaken to Its presence. The truly illumined are those in whom veils in the mind dissolve or become transparent. Spirit is their reality and the only Voice they heed.

Judging by appearances, evil happens. It is absurd to deny it and in some cases catastrophic. To deny evil in the world is escapism, ignorance, or insanity, yet to inwardly accept powers apart from an infinite Intelligence and Love is to become subject to them. Only by experiencing the Self that is one with an infinite Source do we develop a state of consciousness where evil has nothing to cling to. It takes constant practice to bring ourselves out of the physical sense of life into what Jesus called a "kingdom not of this world,"[1] and others describe as a spiritual or Fourth Dimension that is revealed when the ego is out of the way.

The deeper the awareness of spiritual reality, the more we see evils fade in our experience, unless the belief in a physical world is so adamant that it will not yield. It takes a conscious act to bring ourselves into the spiritual dimension. The next time you or a loved one is ill, or someone offends you, rather than react with fear or resentment, pause for a moment and recognize the omnipresence of Spirit. Words of themselves do nothing, but they serve as a wake-up call to enter the stillness where Omnipresence functions. Drop all thought of conditions. Drop all thought of *person* and be still.

It only takes an instant of stillness for Grace to enter the scene. All discords and diseases will not vanish, but when the peace of the spiritual universe permeates our awareness, it changes the outcome in ways we cannot predict. The problem may dissolve, or a solution appear, or we see the person or situation differently. We are seeing the rays of our own enlightened awareness. Those of us dedicated to mystical and metaphysical paths have seen all kinds of negative situations dissolve or diminish, though not always for everyone or all conditions for the same person There is much we do not understand, but we have seen Grace function when we reach a point of perfect peace within ourselves.

Purity of Heart

Illumination happens by Grace, but it takes dedication, purity of heart, and constant practice to stay "up there." Even enlightened individuals are sometimes so entranced or dismayed by an appearance that they lose the vision temporarily, some for the rest of a lifetime. We all suffer the consequences until Spirit reigns in our awareness. Fewer people today worship the concept of a God who could bring world peace and stop crime, disease, and disasters but does not. The real mystery is why people still worship this image and pray for its favors.

Something more is needed to awaken to a Presence that has never stopped bestowing Its love upon all. Many awaken only when faced with a problem for which the world has no solution, and religion offers no solace. As they cry out in the depths of themselves, they break through the belief of separation that blocks the awareness of a Love that never lets go of anyone. Those who experience this Presence witness Grace in amazing ways.

A friend stood on a corner waiting for a bus after attending a meditation group. Suddenly she saw two cars about to collide in front of her. She immediately closed her eyes and felt herself robed in the peace she felt at the meeting we had both attended. There was no time to think a thought, say a prayer, or jump out of the way. A second or two later she opened her eyes, and both cars had safely driven by. It was impossible. The proof was in her voice when she called me right after it happened, although skeptics never believe.

When something happens that is highly improbable or impossible, it is considered luck or coincidence if acknowledged at all. Some who pray for miracles occasionally receive them, but not because a God was persuaded to bless them out of the billions he chooses to ignore. Either someone pure of heart has touched the Infinite in prayer, or the power of the mind has produced an outer effect. Mental power can produce an effect, but does not bring permanent blessings or spiritual transformation.

As individuals spiritually awaken, the world changes one by one. The light spreads one candle at a time. Individual differences are of no consequence when a spiritual impulse governs and universal good comes before personal interests. As more people experience the same Spirit in all, less discordant energy goes into the atmosphere. Human consciousness will be transformed.

Spiritual Discernment Explained

The fabric of the transformed consciousness is impenetrable when we discern Spirit as the *real* presence, power, and life. If this seems too far-fetched, have you ever sensed the magnitude of someone beyond looks, personality, and reputation, perhaps someone you just met, barely knew, or saw from afar? If you have, your spiritual discernment revealed it.

A few years ago a quiet elderly woman attended a meditation group in my home. The moment she stepped in the door, I felt an instant shift in awareness. While others were exchanging quiet greetings, I was lifted into a space of absolute stillness, as if time stopped. I later learned she was raised in Christian Science and had been an Infinite Way student for more than 50 years. It was obvious she had made herself a temple for God. Nothing in her appearance caught my attention; it was her developed consciousness that touched me. It is the Soul of us that recognizes the Soul of others. We spiritually discern the reality of their being with the reality of ours.

Spiritual discernment differs from intuition. Intuition operates on the level of good and evil. We get a positive or negative feeling about someone or something on the temporal plane. It guides us in right directions and helps keep us safe. It reminds us if we forget to lock the door, prompts us to stop in a particular store where there happens to be something we need or desire, and warns us to avoid certain people or situations. Spiritual discernment reveals that which is eternally real and occurs in a moment of Grace. We receive an assurance that we are never alone and revelations of spiritual truth. We sense a person's true being, which is always a surprise for it is nothing like the outer masks of personality, looks, or occupation. Spiritual discernment also dispels evils in the realization that there are none in Spirit.

As our meditations deepen in the awareness of Omnipresence as the only presence, power, and life, our spiritual discernment becomes more active and our intuition keener. We may be led to take actions we had not planned and do nothing where we had planned to take action. Sometimes doing nothing accomplishes far more than anything we could do, for only Spirit is unlimited in Its power and unerring in Its wisdom. Even after a deep spiritual experience, the temporal world may seem more real than the eternal unless we rest often in the awareness that this is a spiritual universe—*all of it*—not part Spirit and part matter. We still see a physical world with our eyes, but we know something more is there. The slightest glimpse is like watching a stone dissolve in our hands, while sensing a Presence that can collapse time and space in an instant. These are experiences in consciousness that express in tangible ways.

It takes constant vigilance to dwell in spiritual awareness because world beliefs pound at our mentality 24 hours a day. Meditation opens the mind to the spiritual landscape and shuts out the debris that is not spiritually real. A spiritual Presence permeates our awareness and transforms our experience. The proof is in the practice.

Try the Waters of Spirit

Anyone can experience Grace who is willing to try the waters of Spirit. It has nothing to do with religious belief, fervor or virtue, but with consciously attuning to the *I* at the center of your being and allowing a spiritual impulse to govern. As the memory of Oneness returns, what seems defective, missing, or discordant begins to fade in the awareness of spiritual wholeness.

The earth will not disappear, but more peace appears in yourself and your world. The cause of distress may not change, but it no longer concerns you, or you may be led to make changes where it no longer affects you. The physical body will not vanish, but when it no longer dominates thought, pains lessen or cease. Death will not come before you fulfill the purpose for which you were born, or spiritually decide it cannot be completed and are ready to move on. Fulfilling a spiritual purpose has nothing to do with human ideals or age. Buddha lived to be 80, but Jesus was only 33 and seemed to have utterly failed when he was crucified. When we depart, it will be like discarding old clothes for which we no longer have a use or desire. We will not look back as we pass on to a grander view of life and of love, and the welcome of those who await us there.

Every time we touch a point of perfect peace within ourselves, we touch the still waters of Spirit that flow through everything. There may have to be many changes in our awareness before Grace takes over in all our ways, but be not dismayed: a divine embrace is always waiting to gather us into the allness of One.

The Allness of One

The allness of One not only runs through everything, *It is everything.* Every right idea, form, and expression can be traced back to the same Source. That is why conscious oneness with God is oneness with all good for all persons, but this only operates in our experience if we are conscious of it. Grace is everyone's inheritance, but awareness is the catalyst that brings it into manifestation.

What we are not conscious of does not function in our experience. People could die of thirst if they did not know fresh water were available, or live in poverty if they knew nothing about a wealthy inheritance. Unless we understand the truth about the nature of God as *I,* indwelling and omnipresent, we do not witness spiritual laws functioning in our lives or world.

The more we acknowledge the allness of One, the more we witness the omnipresence of Grace. It takes practice. Practice on the spiritual path is a denial of everything the ego believes. It begins as a mental discipline, but transformation occurs on a deeper level. When we keep our minds filled with spiritual truth, we become instruments of a Presence that functions in silence and appears in practical ways. It appears in impractical ways too, for there are no barriers to Grace, except the ones we accept in our minds.

Become a channel for Grace by keeping the mind attuned to the *I* at the center of your being, rather than filling it with the world's common denominators. Anyone who recognizes the allness of One can be restored to the fullness of Grace. Inwardly resist nothing, because resistance blocks an inner flow that brings Grace into manifestation. When nothing blocks the peace of God in our awareness, the flow of Grace is inevitable.

Be still, so still
that peace descends like
a robe upon your shoulders,
softer than feathers,
more elusive than air.
That is the cloth
that is tightly woven,
yet transparent and pliable.

Nothing ruffles its threads
or disturbs its patterns.

Be still.
Be alert.
Just BE

12

Essential Points about Grace

And thy people shall be My people—under Grace.

An Inner Voice

When the above words came through in a deep meditation for someone, the first part[1] was familiar, but the last two words gave it a new and immediate meaning. They came through after a pause as part of a rhythm. Words of revelation often come in a rhythm, with pauses as distinct as the words.

Years later the words came with a shock: *The only Grace you will see operating is the Grace realized in your own awareness.* There is no God or Grace "out there" to bless anyone unless it has been realized in our awareness. Spirit is always expressing Its all, but we have to attune to It and accept the Grace that is already given. It starts with acknowledgement but *awareness* or *realization* is a different realm of knowing than intellectual agreement. We have to drop our ideas about God and open ourselves to the Reality Itself.

Before pondering some final points about Grace, pause to rest in the awareness: *Let Thy Spirit bear witness with my Spirit.* Only when Spirit reveals Itself to Itself do we catch the spark that releases Grace into our worlds.

≈ Be still and let your vessel be filled.

≈ Grace has no limits except those we impose in our minds.

≈ Meditation does not initiate Grace. It attunes us to that which always *IS* but has been forgotten.

≈ One person does not have more Grace than another. That is not the nature of God.

≈ You can realize the presence of Grace for anyone, but you cannot change a person's spiritual destiny.

≈ See Grace washing over everyone. Sick or well, rich or poor, alive or dead makes no difference in Spirit.

≈ The moment we feel an inner release, the outer demonstration is complete. The effects may be instantaneous or many details have to fall into place, but the demonstration is already complete—the prayer answered—when the release is felt.

❧ Grace dissolves grief because there is no separation in Spirit. Upon the death of a beloved friend: *You have suffered a great loss, but you have also known a great love. You can choose which emotion to carry.*

❧ Rather than battle appearances and feel overwhelmed, realize you are one with an infinite Love that includes all good for everyone. Then, anchored in the peace of Soul, proceed— one moment, one step, one breath at a time—and watch Grace make the crooked places straight or give you wings to soar above them.

❧ Grace dissolves impenetrable walls, opens the right doors, and blocks the wrong ones. If you manage to push your way through what is not meant for you, it will not be supported by Grace.

❧ If you only dip your toes along the shores of Spirit, that is your measure. If you wade up to your knees, that is your measure. If you insist on clinging to a rope or wearing a life preserver, that is your measure. If you jump in but swim in your own direction, that is your measure. If you do not dive in and let the currents of Grace carry you, you will still be fighting appearances. It is up to you: a little Grace here and there, or the activity of Grace everywhere.

❧ Grace does not mean to do nothing; it means to do nothing of *ourselves*. It means to take time to center ourselves in Soul as the first priority every day, every hour, and discover Grace is carrying us every minute.

❧ Grace never fails.

❧ Spiritual success cannot be judged by contemporary standards. Many great saints, artists, scientists, and innovators were not recognized in their lifetimes. The world had to catch up with their vision before it could see it. Many saw the crucifixion, but only those with spiritual vision saw the resurrection and ascension.

❧ You do not have to believe any of this. Dive into the deep pool of your own being and discover Truth for yourself. Keep trying until you find yourself engulfed in stillness, for *God is in the still, small voice.* You cannot hear it when the mind is shouting.

❧ Rest often in your Soul where there is not a trace of conflict, worry, *dis-ease* or fear. Watch the currents of Grace carry you and those in your awareness. They will have to learn to let Grace carry them too, but Spirit realized is never for self alone. That would be a denial of Omnipresence.

❧ You cannot realize Grace for others without coming under it yourself.

❧ You cannot realize the fullness of Grace for yourself if you leave anyone out.

❧ *And thy people,* those embraced in your realization of Oneness, *shall be My people— under Grace.* There is no greater gift.

❧ We have to be willing to be transformed by the Spirit to come under Grace. It begins with unconditional surrender to Omniscience and the allness of Love, not to human conditions or a punishing God.

❧ You are not here to give love or to receive love, but *to be* love.

❧ When Spirit uses us, It uses us to the highest of our capacities. Imagine creating something as marvelous as *You,* then letting it rust from neglect or misuse or throwing away the best parts. That is not the life by Grace.

❧ Grace is a gift already given. It cannot be "earned" by faith or good works, but multiplies when faith and good works are inspired by the Spirit within us—without ulterior motives.

❧ There is nothing anyone can do to make Grace happen. Even Jesus said he could do *nothing of himself.*[2] Nothing! Do you think he lied?

❧ We do not choose our spiritual teachers or close relationships; we recognize them. It has to do with an internal persuasion, spiritual frequencies, and individual receptivity.

❧ When the right spiritual note plays for us, it resonates within us. We don't have to think about it: the Soul resonates.

❧ To come under Grace does not take time or a deeper understanding. It takes only an instant of awareness—*this instant.* Be still.

❧ Freedom comes with the realization: *I* in Thee and Thou in Me. Nothing else *IS. Only I — forever — Am.*

❧ As a still, soft Voice once said within me:

> Come into My garden,
> I'll let you awhile,
> But only awhile
> For it's full with Me
> And won't fit thee,
> But if you come
> And find just One,
> Oh, come into My garden
> And stay awhile,
> Find that smile
> Of One, oh come!

ADDENDUM:
Three Lessons from
an Inner Voice

These three lessons were given to me by an inner Voice in 2010. I had just begun taking a shower when I heard the words: *We have all died before, but many do not know. There is no better time than now to write it down.* As the words continued to flow, I knew I had to immediately write them down or they would be lost. The second and third message followed within a month. It is another example of the importance of being inwardly alert and willing to stop what we are doing to listen.

I

An Impartation on Dying

We have all died before, but many do not know. There is no better time than now to write it down. Many walk among you who, like you, *know.* They make no claim of resurrection, yet know they had a glimpse of the Eternal and returned to walk the earth, not yet complete. Think now of times you almost died but something saved you: the car that almost struck yours but did not, or sickness that nearly swept your life away.

Some of you remember leaving the shell called body and returning. There were times you almost left but chose to stay, always for a greater purpose than yourself alone. You do not leave until you agree to go, though it does not seem that way to those who know not their Soul. The mind is not the part that knows the Spirit; Soul is that which is of God and knows.

Some have heard the music of the spheres or seen a shining light or felt a cloak of peace that dissolved the pain. It is their wakening to Me that pierced a veil of darkness to let in Truth. Give not yourself to error again, but lift your vision to That which is unseen, unheard in all the tumult of the world. I come again in each to show the way. It has been shown since ancient times, still unacknowledged by those whose eyes are veiled. The ancients knew a higher Being and left records thought false idols by the blind, some now discovered, some lying deep in caves as yet unfound. No less the call that draws them to the search, than the call that any scribe or mystic heard to write it down.

Unrecognized the One that calls all seekers and inspires inspiration in all fields. They fulfill their function who do not use their gifts for self-acclaim or to profit themselves by debasing the loveliness of all. God knows no time or veil to block Its rays, but men shut their minds and keep them out. False gods were made when there is only One. Forget the forms, the concepts that imprison, and find instead the freedom that is yours to claim, for it is Mine and therefore part of all.

No one walks the earth alone in spite of how it seems. The arms of Love reach out to all in forms invisible, as well as those you meet who share your time on earth. Judge not the form, the face or mind, but see instead the Spirit that is the life. It knows no death. Each stays until it has done all it can or wills to do. Each lives again for no one fails to fulfill a purpose that may not culminate this time. They come again, and each life span provides the opportunities to reach a higher place where the Light may shine more fully as their own.

II
A Gift Always Returns

To give is to receive the gift that you have given. It does not seem that way because a gift is often given to control, or to assuage an ego that helps its brother without the love that knows who its brother is. The greater gift is knowing who your brother is, while offering a helping handout when you can.

The gift always returns, though gift you think it not. It may be a distortion of the love you refused to give, or a bliss you never dreamed from love you gave away. It will return in the manner it was bestowed, though the form may differ, for nothing happens outside the self who sent it forth. There is no way to separate the self from what it gives, for giving remains within the circumference that you are. Those who give not, give not to themselves, then wonder why life withholds from them its gifts. All was given to each before a birth that is not a beginning, and the gifts not found unless they are expressed.

Your gifts touch others in ways you do not know; sometimes the slightest warmth inspires a broken life. The opposite is also true: to ignore a person's need can cause a pain you could have eased. How easy to give a smile and lift a humble soul to future greatness, whose life might be a burden and death a wish. You never know a person by the face presented. Think not you do.

The question many face is how to give, not why, for often it seems their store is sparse. Begin to pour what you already have is the lesson taught by all who knew, yet something keeps the cap on and blocks the flow. You think you have not enough and never do increase your giving, for the more you have, the more you spend and find yourself impoverished. What you give *not* is sure to give not back to you, though time may pass before your lack returns. They lack the most who give not outside their closest sphere, which becomes their prison when infinity was given all to live.

Pour what you have: a smile to a stranger on the

street; a kind word or deed; a meal, a gift, a check to feed a hungry soul and body. Pass not by where deprivation seems to rule. Pour with no thought of a return except to bless, grateful for the abundance that allows your giving. The blessings that you give with no demands return in future times to bless you more. Hold not locked up within yourself your gifts or find yourself deprived, for all was given you to help you thrive.

Giving is the Soul's outreach, the extension of who and what you are. Spirit has no boundaries, for infinite Its reach. Think not of what to get but only, "What can I give or share today." Ask and the answer will come—if not within yourself, a person or situation will present. The highest giving is unspoken, when the listening ear receives and releases Grace into the world of time and space. Then God will give Its blessings near and far, but be not fooled: it does not mean to withhold the gifts that are yours to share.

The measure of the gift is not its size, amount or value, but intent. When given out of love beyond your own, that love will bring to others and to you more than yours could ever do. The gift always returns as *more*, for multiplication is the law of increase: good and bad. To give only to those you love with nothing for the rest is to restrict the Soul in its expression and be bound. In truth all who have ever lived are part of you, and what you hold back holds back yourself as well.

If when you read this your life seems dark or bleak, look deeper and ask: What can I give today? Feel love where animosity once reigned; give joy where sadness tries to rule; forgive, and let all grudges go. Give patience when yours is sorely tried, and be a friend to all without the judgments that turn religions into hate. The highest gift is to be still enough to reach the One that pours Its grace to heal broken hearts and bodies and those who welcome death before its time has come.

Let's talk about the infinite One you are, whose reaches go beyond what you know in time and space. Let not today restrict your giving and forgiving what happened in the past. Love all who suffered then as well as now, nor let today restrict your giving and forgiving in the future. You know not what is yet to come but Love knows all, nor does a gift fade in time when truly given. It remains to embrace all who fall and turn to Me; they find a Love to lift their hearts and soar. No one so lifted fails to share their gifts, however great or small. No matter how it seems in the world's eyes, they have all who give their all and *know*.

Receive the gift of Truth and let it flow. Silently it flies like birds to find a home where hearts are open. What gifts you have received, you once have given. What gifts remain withheld, you have withheld. Give now your heart completely where you are, and find your gifts returning near and far.

III

The Prayer that Moves Mountains

Prayer is not of the mind but of the will: a will attuned to Mine will open doors. A listening mind will take you there, where angels dwell and your true home is found. "Be still my mind and hear" is the only prayer worth uttering, the only one where God can find a home to fill. The words that people utter to an idol they conceived bring no response unless the heart is open. Then words can take you as steps upon a ladder to ascend to realms where Love alone exists. There is but love in the will that is of God, the rhythm of a universe unseen.

To think you know the answer to your prayer is to declare your mind knows more than Mine. Idolatry appears in many forms. The mind you claim as yours is not as it may seem. There is only One that knows the best for all. That Mind is yours when you align yourself with Mine. Omniscience reigns wherever *I* am heard, the *I* of you found in the depths of Soul.

Omniscience reigns when you remove the blinders you have put upon yourself to block the truth. Unplug the inner ear and trust the Self that made you who you are. You think you do, but you cannot trust a Self you do not know. Rest from your thoughts, and ask to know the truth you need each day. God's voice is always speaking but only heard in stillness where an inner ear responds.

One Self, One Mind, One Being is true of all. The substance is the same though not the forms. To pray is to reach the place where Grace is touched and carries you on currents to your good. The Light is always there to lead, dissolve or shine as what you need. *Be still, my heart, and know.* Be still brings into being that which knows and *is* the answer to all prayers: the Power that exists behind all form. Then mountains faced will move for you or tunnels open up to take you through. The prayer that moves a mountain does exist. No mountain moves unless God's grace is there.

The quakes that strike your body, mind, and earth are not of God, who holds creation in Its arms, arms that fill Infinity with love. "Consider the birds," but you do not. They worry not and are provided for. You say the words but learn not the lessons I came to teach. I came many times in many forms in all who shared the Light and taught the truth of One. That One is always near to lift a broken heart and fill a lack where none exists in God.

You think amiss and your prayer no longer prays, no longer worships Me in one and all. Lift into Love the enemy, the animal, the beast, and you will see lions lie down with lambs, or their beastliness return to knock them down. No God exists who punishes Its own, but punishment is the law of cruelty and strife. No paramount religion does exist: Spirit is the same in one and all. To listen to the utmost in yourself is to find true prayer and unite yourself with God. Communion first is felt a joy, till none communes for only One is there and you an empty vessel filled to overflowing.

Let this prayer fill the heavens and the earth:

Be still my heart and know.

Be still, my heart, and know.

Be still, my heart.

Be still.

Be

Make spaces for this hymn to ring the world with chimes unheard—beneath all sound a silent song—and watch what happens when My peace takes form. Then truly God is born again on earth. Judge not the forms but see the One in all, and watch your prayers move mountains large and small.

Acknowledgments

With a grateful heart to the following persons for their contributions to this book:

My son Jonathan Mork, for taking the time to read many drafts, encouraging me to persist, and helping me to focus. Without his guidance, vision, and support, this book would not have been written.

Lilian de Arias, whose home was a temple of Truth in London, for her spiritual insights as she worked closely with me to edit the manuscript, finishing days before she swam into "the arms of God" and greater glory.

My sons: Jeremy Mork, whose spiritual healing as an infant and experience of the Light are recorded in this book; and Dempsey Patrick Mork, who lived only 10 years and taught me the fallacy of religions that limit God to their own beliefs.

For their critiques of early chapters and different perspectives:

Gail Felicetta, who experiences her deepest truth in the wilderness, for her grammatical expertise, enduring friendship since high school, and ever-cheerful heart.

Reverend Richard Kingsley, whose dedication to Truth remained up to his death, which he knew was yet another new beginning.

Marny Trounson, who travels the same spiritual path, for her helpful comments and her clarity on the freedom of a true teacher/student relationship.

My sister Pene Zarnoti, a practicing Catholic, who gives of herself without hesitation and has witnessed many miracles of Grace in her life.

Writer friend Pat Erickson, a free spirit not inclined to books of this genre, who kept me grounded and whose memoir has been an inspiration.

I want to thank Michael Krupp for taking the time to read my manuscript and encouraging me to publish it.

I also want to honor my spiritual teachers (in chronological order): Joel S. Goldsmith, whom I never met in the flesh; Lorraine Sinkler, Luella Overeem, Virginia Stephenson, and Joy Powell. Their developed spiritual awareness dispelled many dark nights, like bubbles popping in mid-air, with unmistakable evidence of a higher Love.

And especially the invisible Presence that has impelled, guided, and revealed what I could not have known, witnessed, or done of myself and is present within everyone.

Endnotes

Note: All Bible quotations are from the King James version, unless noted below. Often the words heard in meditation slightly differ, but references found in the Bible or other sources are cited. No punctuation at the end of a meditation or poem is intentional, for what is eternal is without end.

INTRODUCTION: A Spiritual Awakening

1. Brother Lawrence, 17th-century mystic, *The Practice of the Presence of God,* "Fourth Conversation," first English translation, many editions.

2. Treatment today usually prevents Rh disease, caused when an Rh-negative mother and Rh-positive father conceive an Rh-positive baby. If the fetus's blood cells get into the mother's bloodstream, her body produces antibodies to fight them. It can cause jaundice, anemia, brain damage, heart failure and death in the fetus. In later pregnancies with an Rh-positive baby, the risks increase.

3. John 14:11
4. John 14:28
5. Joel S. Goldsmith, 20th century mystic (1892-1964), spiritual teacher, healing practitioner, and author of 50 books, published by Acropolis Books (acropolisbooks.com), available from Amazon and local book sources. Recordings of his classes are available from joelgoldsmith.com.

Ch. 1: The Path of Oneness
1. Ralph Waldo Emerson, "Essay on Experience," 1844.

Ch. 2: Unto Ourselves
1. John 20: 22-23, DRA
2. 1 Kings, 19:12

Ch. 3: A Divine Persuasion
1. "Porch Prayer" found on a card in St. Lawrence Church in Winchester, England. Formerly engraved on doors of some old churches of the Church of England.
2. Luke 11:52
3. More than 50 Gnostic texts from the 3rd and 4th centuries AD; discovered in 1945 in a cave near Nag Hammadi, Egypt. Believed destroyed when the Church condemned all non-canonical books. Also referred to as the secret or lost books of the Bible.
4. John 16:7

5. Matthew: 5:39

Ch. 5: Always Speaking
1. Quote later found in Revelation 19:6

Ch. 6: Resting in Spirit
1. Matthew 19:26

Ch. 7: 100 Percent Spirit
1. Chapter IX: "What About This Body," *The Art of Spiritual Healing,* copyright ©1959 by Joel S. Goldsmith, renewed in 1975 by Emma A. Goldsmith with reprint rights granted to Acropolis Books, Publisher, under its I-Level imprint, under a reprint arrangement with HarperCollins Publishers.

Ch. 8: A New Dawn
1. Hebrews 13:2
2. John 16:33

Ch. 9: Our Spiritual Orbit
1. John 6:37

Chapter 10: The Power of Prayer
1. John 14:6

Chapter 11: The Cloth is Tightly Woven
1. John 18:36

Chapter 12: Essential Points about Grace
1. Ruth 1:1
2. John 5:30-32; 8:28

CPSIA information can be obtained
at www.ICGtesting.com
Printed in the USA
LVOW04s1318141016
508795LV00018B/404/P